RAISING TIP TOP KIDS IN A TOPSY-TURVY WORLD

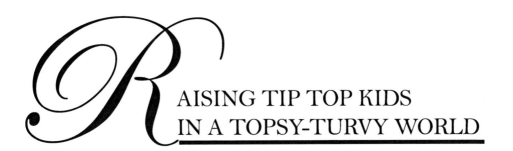

RAISING TIP TOP KIDS
IN A TOPSY-TURVY WORLD

Linda Roblee

Outskirts Press, Inc.
Denver, Colorado

The opinions expressed in this manuscript are solely the opinions of the author and do not represent the opinions or thoughts of the publisher. The author has represented and warranted full ownership and/or legal right to publish all the materials in this book.

Outskirts Press, Inc.
http://www.outskirtspress.com

ISBN: 978-1-4327-4568-4

Outskirts Press and the "OP" logo are trademarks belonging to Outskirts Press, Inc.

PRINTED IN THE UNITED STATES OF AMERICA

DEDICATION

For Melissa, Kevin, Katie, Randy, Kathy, Andrew, David and Rodney.
And for John and Ricky who've gone on ahead.
If I had it to do all over again, I would.

For Doug and Stephen, who began and finished my "Why's."

And for my parents,
Who gave me the freedom, though often with raised eyebrows,
To be myself when that was not always easy for any of us.

Oh, and for the grandchildren and great grandchildren, here and yet to come,
who are sweet frosting on my cake.

Linda Roblee

July, 2009

TABLE OF CONTENTS

INTRODUCTION

"You must have done SOMETHING right!"

This book is about my family. Well, that is PART of what this book is about. It's really about life as it has passed through the filter of my mind and experiences. And really, it's about the mercy of God and of His love for my children.

Most of the principles I accepted over the years were learned "on the job." And they seem as valid to me today, now that my children are grown and have their own children, as they did while I was more actively learning how to be a Christian mom, wife and friend. With that in mind, I'll share life principles (and experiences) that have proven themselves treasures to me.

One afternoon approximately twenty years ago, my daughter-in-law Tammy and I sat at my kitchen table while her two tiny girls played noisily around our feet. Stirring her coffee and smiling, Tammy said, "Mom, you're my role model when it comes to mothering!"

I must have shown my surprise, because she laughed as she continued. It was a real shock, for no one knew better than I my own limitations. I never considered myself an "example" in any of my many roles in life. A role model? ME?! I don't think so!

I was there, and I remember that I was imperfect. Suddenly, visions of my domestic inadequacies began to flash through my mind. I'm the lady who most days remembered to take meat for dinner out of the freezer each afternoon, the moment the first kid home from school ran through the door, yelling hungrily, "Hi, Mom! ... What's for supper!?" I'm the same woman who started the water in the laundry, then absent-mindedly ran off to answer the door or the telephone, mediate a conflict over a toy, wipe a dirty face, or ... you get it... and just HAPPENED to walk by the washer some minutes later in time to find that the entire washing cycle had run soapless, lid open, without one piece of clothing in it! If Tammy meant a mother's domestic efficiency and organization, I was never the obvious choice for role model of ANY year! My domestic deficiencies had always been more than slightly obvious!

Even as a teenager, I was often barred from using mother's kitchen because of the damage I could inflict during "inspired" late night baking binges. I had already begun a lifetime of nocturnal creativity. It just never occurred to me to think that other people might find it difficult to sleep peacefully with the aroma of freshly baked goodies, the noise of mixing spoons tapping edges of metal bowls, or an occasional Broadway song lyric bursting full volume, from my suddenly domestic lips.

Years later, looking at my own kitchen counters filled with the remnants of my own adolescent bakers -- pans, bowls, etc., that "wouldn't fit in the dishwasher, Mom!" I had a tremendous empathy for my mother. And somehow, I think if she had seen my own kitchen clutter, she would have laughed with that one eyebrow raised knowingly, at the wonderful justice in the world!

And, so, knowing full well my own domestic inadequacies, I remember looking across the table at my young daughter-in-law who admired my "mothering," apparently quite sincere in her comments, and asked with some astonishment, "Really? Why?"

"Well," she said, "when my girls grow up, I want to have the same kind of relationship with them you have with your kids. You seem to really enjoy each other. They talk to you about nearly anything. They really trust you. And so do I."

OH!!!... it wasn't about domestic order! That wasn't my accomplishment! Tammy was talking about the REAL stuff! The communication! She admired the relationships she witnessed. Come to think of it, so did I!

It was time out for a tissue, and a hug from a "mom by marriage" whose heart seemed full, warmed and thankful. Later that night, I began to ask myself how it had happened. How had I been so blessed to be friends as well as mother to my family?

The years passed. Tammy was a wonderfully supportive mother for her daughters who grew into beautiful, open-hearted young women. Though we were separated by miles and divorce and the re-formation of modern families that occur after divorce, Tammy and I continued to love and trust each other. And that day allowed me continued opportunity to evaluate my life as a mother.

Over the years, that moment and those words from my first daughter-in-law have been one of the sweetest complements of my life. There's been so much water under (and over) that bridge that the bridge has been washed out a couple of times since then.

Though all the kids are gone from my nest, and I live alone with my two little dogs, I still don't get all the laundry, cooking, cleaning, organizing, etc, done as well as I should. And since I've grown older, I find it reassuring that among the things I've misplaced around here is the measuring stick for judging perfect models of just about anything! I stopped worrying quite a long while ago about being perfect. And these days, I'm more content with being REAL.

Of course, Tammy wasn't talking about the things I did or

didn't do. She was talking about RELATIONSHIPS. And that's, hopefully, the important thing about being a Mom. Or, for that matter, about being a PERSON. Who we are is more dependent upon our relationships with God, our family, and others, than on our DOING things well.

Even now, thank goodness, it's pretty much true that my kids generally liked me. And I liked them most of the time -- still do, as a matter of fact! Loving isn't the hard part. It's LIKING that sometimes gets tough. I am thankful that my kids grew into neat people -- sometimes in spite of their mother's influences. Still, like the kid in the old Shake'n'Bake television commercial used to holler, sometimes I also want to shout, "I helped!" There are some neat young adults in the world, whose inner security system and very best qualities grew stronger in the love and acceptance of my home. Today, I sincerely believe that if they were not my own children, now grown, I would want them for my <u>friends</u>. And who could ask for a better reward as a parent?

Continued relationships with other people I've loved, not only my family, but former students, as well as old and new friends and coworkers, continue to encourage me, even though often without thought or planning, that somewhere along the way, I <u>must</u> have done <u>something</u> right.

Tammy's compliment started me thinking about what it takes to raise good kids... meaning, grown up people you'd treasure as friends. As I began to work through my own "system," I began to record my thoughts.

Each achievement, be it a race won, or a beautiful garden harvested, or a satisfying long-term relationship, begins with a moment called "START." We see the goal in our minds. We understand the steps necessary in order to finish with the results we want. But sitting and fantasizing about our future achievements and rewards will not bring the rewards. Somewhere, some time, we must BEGIN, follow the course set before us, and then keep going until we reach that goal.

The words that follow are intended to be a BEGINNING for those who are starting their individual or family life-long marathons, or for those parents who are "in process," and sometimes look for some encouragement. And I believe that many of the ideas could be helpful to teachers, counselors, ministers, and others of us who assist young people mature. Though this project was originally conceived as a gift for my own adult children, I share it with love, with those who are drawn to it.

You may wonder, "Who IS this woman? What are her special qualifications for telling me how to help young people?" That's fair. I hope that by the time you finish reading, you'll have a good understanding of who I am -- REALLY am.

At the moment, I am a high school English and Drama teacher, involved with teens nearly every day of my adult life for many years. I am also a parent and grandparent. My husband and I birthed three lovely children together, adopted six more, and foster-parented about fifteen other children. Hopefully, though our 23-year-old marriage eventually ended in divorce, much of the good that came from our love and respect for each other and our efforts together will survive for a very long time.

As I look back over the years, I realize that there were certain important principles that I learned both by study, and "on the job," that might be helpful in the lives of my grandchildren. There were also lessons and thoughts that I'm certain I may not have taken the time to talk about clearly with my young kids because, to tell you truth, I was too busy trying to deal with each day's challenges. As a matter of fact, it is very likely that my grown children may have never heard either my husband or me explain much about our choices at various moments in our lives together. You know how it is -- the fireman is so busy putting out the little brush fires that he can't talk about the principles by which he's working to save the forest.

Perhaps there are others who will benefit from the telling, as well. I will try to make it enjoyable as well as instructional, for I have spent more hours of my life smiling than frowning. And, unlike so much unwanted advice, I offer these principles to be weighed, evaluated, and perhaps modified and used, as you wish, Dear Reader. Freely, without fear, I share my experiences and lessons with you. From one generation of "firefighters" to another generation, here's what I believe, why I believe it, and how it has worked in my life.

Who is this woman?

I have been a wife, a mother, an actress, a student, a humorist, a writer, a lover, a public speaker, both a fulfilled believer and a discontented seeker after all that life has to offer.

I once traveled in India, and saw poverty there that was an assault to every human sense, and a wondrous beauty that changed my life forever.

I laugh often and freely at the antics of children and at grown people who have, at least occasionally, allowed the child inside to "play" again.

I nearly died of malaria while living in the United States, surrounded by doctors who had never before seen the disease.

I have met and loved and wept for some of the most interesting people God ever created.

I have held a dying child in my arms, and have dressed a newborn baby.

I have listened, enchanted, to the stories of old people.

I have loved people of different races and cultures and have felt richer in their love returned.

I have learned to believe that not only is there a God, but that He is intimately concerned about people in this world.

I have been considered wealthy by some, and I have been poor. And I have been passionately happy at both times.

Who am I to tell you what I have learned about life? I am a woman, rather like my grandmother, whose working hands pieced together beautiful quilts from the remnants of fabric she accumulated, gifts for those she loved.

Instead, I, a teacher and philosopher, a storyteller, a passionate lover of life, have woven together the remnants of my varied experiences into a story that is more than just a story -- one that I pray will be a comfort and help for you, my beloved children, whom I hug with my heart.

CHAPTER 1

"In the beginning..."

When Rod and I married in 1966, neither of us imagined we'd eventually have a family large enough that a family "car" meant a twelve-passenger bus! Over our 20-plus years together, Rod and I cared for our nine "regular" birth and adopted kids, plus many other "kinda" (meaning, foster, temporary or "kinda ours") kids. Originally, both of us loved kids, or at least the IDEA of kids. I was a high school English and Drama teacher who'd been an only child until my one sister was born when I was thirteen. In my small, tightly-knit, somewhat private family, I had always been, to the alternating consternation and pride of my parents, the most verbal, demonstrative, and independent of the lot.

Rod also had one sister in the middle of an enormous extended family of aunts, uncles and cousins numbering greater than the armies of some small countries, it seemed to me! They were a loud, warm-hearted, loyal, delightfully German family, and I had quite a time learning and remembering all the names those first few years.

With his large extended family, it was not always necessary to explain yourself — they seemed to accept each other and even the newcomer freely. Finding one's place in the group also never seemed a major issue. You were welcome to fit in wherever you felt comfortable and stay as long as you wished. I suspect Rod never really wondered, "Who am I? Where do I belong?" He just seemed to know.

When I was a little girl, near 9 or 10 years old, one of my mom's favorite cousins visited our small Nebraska hometown all the way from California. He was a very pleasant man with dark red hair, a warm smile and contagious chuckle. One evening, in the middle of his mother, Great Aunt Mattie's kitchen, reminiscent of *The Waltons*, surrounded by a room filled with chatting adults, Dwayne bent down and asked me, "Well, Linda, how many children do you want to have when you grow up?"

I suppose it was a simple way to begin a conversation with a little girl one hardly knew, the only child in a room of adults enjoying grown up talk. I can picture it now, as it seemed nearly all the adults stopped talking to one another and listened, amused, for the answer. I see her, without hesitation, a little girl who was used to the company of adults, standing with long golden curls, blue eyes, and an openness that would eventually lead her into all sorts of adventures and misadventures.

"Twenty-five."

It seemed to me that all the grownups smiled knowingly and chuckled at my answer, and I remember that they winked at one another, agreeing that I would feel differently after "she actually has a few children of her own."

I suppose, knowing some of their family histories, I can understand their doubt. These great aunts and uncles had lived through the Great Depression, several world wars, and years of concern about raising their children. Who among them would have wished for 25 kids?! They doubted my childish dream with good reason. And I imagine few of them ever remembered the short exchange.

But...I remembered. It was another one of those important moments of my life. And it remained true. These many years later, I know that idealistic, optimistic, wide-eyed little girl was right. She knew then what was important to her. Even then.

I had just finished reading Louisa May Alcott's *Little Women* and identified myself with the character Jo, who grew up to be a writer and took in children who were without families. I remember the ache for companionship in an only child's heart. My early dreams were often of kids, some of them unwanted by anybody else, and living with them in a big old refurbished house, and being the mother of a family put together from different beginnings. I would write, and I would be a mother to many children

This dream as an ideal still lives in me. So does the child.

Over the growing up years, I wrote, acted, dreamed, imagined, and fought against the loneliness in my life with many very good friendships and activities of youth. But always, there was this sense of destiny and purpose that I didn't quite understand -- couldn't quite put into words. I remember throughout my life thinking, "I KNOW I was created for a purpose, and someday I will know what it is."

At the age of 13, I became, at last, a big sister. It was a wonderful time. I remember the joy of hurrying home from school each day to see how much my baby sister had grown and changed. What fun it was to see her learn new things. My mom and I often laughed that Lori might not have known which one of us was her mom for her first few years, because when I was home, she was usually with me! It would be difficult to say which of us was influenced more by that early relationship. But it was a wonderful time.

Later, during my final semester in college, when I met a young man just returned from Viet Nam, a man who was obviously kind and family-oriented, I was probably nearly as idealistic as that little girl standing in the middle of Aunt Mattie's kitchen floor. I guess we both were. At the time we met, though I had been nearly crushed in spirit by a personal loss that left me aching and empty, meeting a good and lovely young man, soon gave me renewed hope for a future.

We agreed on just about every important thing, or so it seemed. As I look back at it now, very likely the ideas about home and family, which I so freely shared with him, had not occurred to him, or certainly not been spoken by him, and so he found it easy to nod and agree with me. He was quiet, calm, and kind, with the most beautiful smile! His acceptance and almost immediate love for me began a healing of my often shaky self esteem that took many turns in the years that followed.

We married quickly -- three months and three days after we met. He was what I was looking for, and I guess I was the same for him. Soon some very obvious differences in our interests and personalities were overshadowed by our mutual desire to create a warm, secure and loving family and for quite some time I felt quite content. I taught high school for two years. Rod went to technical school, and we began planning and building a life together. I finally had the yellow kitchen I'd always fantasized about, and I delighted in each part of the domestic picture puzzle we put in place. Of course, there were always those little nagging domestic accidents, like the time I put something new and <u>red</u> in the wash that colored all our white underwear, and especially Rod's favorite plaid shirt, PINK! But we laughed, he wore it proudly, and we went on.

Two years after our wedding, I quit teaching to become a full-time mommy for our first daughter, Melissa. No baby could have been more welcome. She was a wonderful baby and toddler, filling my days with the adventures, at last, of being the mommy that I'd long anticipated. I saw and even admired her strong personality as she grew increasingly independent, with those tight blonde curls bouncing as she ran through each waking hour, full of spirit, sparkle and hugs. Bright, eager, and delightful, she was always interested in being my helper.

When Melissa, then called "Missy," was 13 months old, we were equally thrilled with our baby son, Kevin, who came with a full head of dark red hair and a keen awareness of everything around him. He seemed more responsive to colors, scents, and even to words unspoken. He became Missy's "pet," the center of a lifetime of doting that may have opened her interests, through helping others, into the medical world.

Most of the time when they were small, Melissa and Kevin were inseparable. I have photos of them happily decorating trays of sugar cookies, of her giving him a ride in her doll buggy, and 3-year-old Missy painting 2-year-old Kevin's fingernails while he sat patiently, grinning at the camera, unaware that REAL men didn't wear pink fingernail polish! Though most of their time together, she rescued him, occasionally he had to step in as the "brother."

One morning, after a Nebraska Spring rain they were out riding squeaky tricycles along the sidewalk in the fenced-in yard while I prepared lunch. We lived at that time, on the family farm homestead, and Rod had used his new backhoe the day before the rain, to dig an 8 or 10 foot wide, relatively shallow rectangular pit outside our fenced yard, ostensibly to bury trash.

The kids, seeing the bright sunny morning, wanted to play outside, so we put on lightweight jackets and their boots, and let them go outside to play, with orders to stay inside the fenced yard. I could hear their squeaking tricycles rolling back and forth, checked out the kitchen window about every two minutes, and ran outside to see where they were when they suddenly became quiet or disappeared out of sight around the front of the house. Suddenly, probably 2 or 3 minutes after the last check, Kevin, then two, came running in the back door shouting excitedly, "Mommy, Mommy! Missi TUCK!"

Frightened, I tore out the door, and followed him towards the loud hollering that told me she was REALLY angry more than hurt – from outside the gate, around the garage, to where our German shepherd, Princess, stood calmly looking down at a furious Missy, who had somehow slipped down into Daddy's trash trench, and stood anchored firmly in about two inches of muddy water. I got down on my knees, grabbed her gooey hands, pulled her out, none the worse for sliding down the muddy bank, but as "mad as a wet hen" that her new red boots were stuck in the mud below, and that she'd not been able to get out by herself. It seems to me that after that day, when I told her to stay in the yard, she did.

Three years after Kevin's arrival, our last birth child, Kathryn (who has NEVER COMPLETELY outgrown being "Katie!") joined our lively little troop. She was a beautiful, patient baby, and we five were very busy and usually quite happy together. I threw myself into the "Motherhood March" as intensely as I had every other activity of my life, and only rarely noticed a twinge of the "aloneness" that had been my lifelong enemy. There simply wasn't time!

I suppose a normal couple would have been content with these three lovely children. We were quite happy, but there always seemed to be "room for one more!" Obviously, I was still working off the *Little Women* character of Jo.

Before long, we began taking in foster teens. I had taught teens for two years before Melissa's birth, and it seemed natural to have them around. Some people seemed to think that bringing more children into our family meant taking, or stealing, something from our three birth children. Even before we took other children into our lives, we believed that adding the love of other family members was simply addition. If there were increased expenses, they were not as important as the multiplied benefits of a larger family.

What a larger family might miss in money and material goods would certainly be compensated for with other, more important benefits. Time has not altered my belief. There are financial, emotional and psychological costs that should be weighed, of course, before enlarging one's household, but I can imagine no better way to live than what I've chosen.

I've often wondered if the choices we made at that time were "ours" or just MINE. I know that I'm idealistic and ambitious, and that when I believe something, I can be quite persuasive. I also know that my husband loved me and wanted me to be happy, and it is a very strong possibility that had the decisions been more his than mine, we might have lived a different life.

At any rate, by the time Katie was two years old, we had begun receiving children for foster and, later, adoptive care. In the next few years, we added Ricky, who was at five years old, labeled "retarded." Ricky, with unshackled acceptance, love and affection for others, probably had more influence on our family than any other single person. Many times I have looked back at those busy, wonderful, sometimes overwhelming days, and at the "family Ricky built." I'll share more about Ricky's life and special kids later.

After sheltering a number of teenaged foster children for brief periods of time, we were asked to take Randy, who, at 15, was a boy social workers said, "Just needs a family to believe in him." When we met Randy, we also fell in love with his younger sister, Kathy, 12, and John, who had his tenth birthday shortly after coming home to live with us. Eventually, adoption allowed all four —Ricky, Randy, Kathy and John-- to become officially ours. What a memorable experience! I remember riding home from court on the day Randy, Kathy and John were adopted, and John asking if he should tell the teachers at school to reseat him in their seating arrangements, "because I have a new name now."

Eight years after Melissa's birth, we adopted twin babies, Andrew and David, who were, for all of us, like "frosting on a pop tart!" Throughout the years, we had other young people, various friends, relatives, and even a few family units, staying in our home from a matter of days to as long as one or two years. It was a big house, filled with life, filled with occasional noise, to be sure, but mostly filled with love and acceptance.

The Bible has much to say about children, but probably Psalms 127 says it as wonderfully as any other scripture in verses 3 to 5: "Behold, children are a heritage from the Lord, the fruit of the womb a reward. As arrows are in the hand of a warrior, so are children of one's youth. Happy, blessed and fortunate is the man whose quiver is filled with them." (Amplified Version)

When our children were young, it was probably most entertaining for visitors to observe our family during meal time. In fact, I have known people who drove MILES to see us in action! Probably much like the Ma and Pa Kettle movies I remember from my childhood, mealtime began with everyone shuffling into place on the benches beside our long harvest table, and bowing their heads for a quick prayer. Meal time was filled with conversation, laughter and not much ceremony. I guess the German Grandma in me believed then, and to a certain extent, now, that a full table, a full stomach, and a full home indicate a full heart. Even today when it's considerably more uncommon to see all my children together around any table, my happiest times are surrounded by them and their noisy interaction.

I remember the joy I felt some 20 years after my wedding, sitting at the foot of the table for a family birthday celebration, and listening and watching as sixteen members of our IMMEDIATE family ate together. We all missed Ricky, who had died a few years earlier, but each of us had a few funny and tender "Ricky stories" and the memory of his warmth and joy, to keep him connected to us. Kevin, John and Randy laughingly told about some adventure that had been previously unknown by their parents. The grown boys still teased their sisters, and the sisters, now aunts, helped the mommies with the babies. I could see that some of our cherished family traditions were still intact. Good food, good fun and lots of laughter.

That day, all the kids teased their father about his receding hairline and enlarging waistline. They teased me about something I forgot to bring to the table (usually the bread!). Randy still ate three helpings! Kevin flexed his muscles for all to see. Katie ran to answer the telephone. Kathy held one of the babies on her lap and grinned at her silly brothers. Melissa noticed something that needed to be done, and jumped to do it. John told a corny joke, quoting the dialogue from a favorite old movie that no one else could have remembered. The twins competed with each other over something, and probably nothing in particular! I sat, surrounded by those I love most in the world, and marveled that Rod and I, a couple whose marriage, even in its beginning, had probably very little chance of survival, had yet somehow managed to parent fairly peacefully, this bustling, assorted group of unique people – a put-together family. How did two rather unlikely people like us marry and grow a family of neat, loving people?

How did it happen? And how could we be so blessed?

Early in our married life, Rod and I didn't spend a great deal of time formulating a philosophy of childrearing. (Our lack of real communication and mutual trust probably eventually destroyed the strength of our early relationship. But that's a later story.) Early on, we did not have a "master plan" for developing the family of which we are now so proud. Even now, I wonder what characteristics within the two of us individually, or shared between us, accounted for the amazing cohesiveness of a group of people who were joined together by love rather than blood?

We were certainly a mismatched pair, young and idealistic, who were willing to try with all our hearts to live what we believed. And that's probably where it starts. In all areas of life, success comes to those who live what they believe.

So, am I about to tell you what to believe? Well, not EXACTLY! I will share my beliefs, because that's where it all begins. Then I encourage you to check your own beliefs for yourself, and then you will hopefully choose to be absolutely faithful to them.

CHAPTER 2

"The Heart of All Things"

Every person who ever lived has a religion. At the center of each life, there is a belief system that governs our every thought, every action, every decision. Whatever you believe in as right or wrong, adhere to in making choices, return to for comfort in times of pain --that is your religion.

That's why I believe that every person has a religion. Yes, I mean everyone. And if each person isn't "given" a god to believe in, he or she may spend years searching for something or someone to believe in 100%. It's part of our nature.

Even the person who has the most complacent attitude about formal religion (organized churches, etc.) has a strong set of principles that he or she depends upon. That particular person may put his hopes in a system of government; or he may consider the fulfillment of personal goals more important than everything else; or he may live to pursue intellectual inquiry, or his own immediate physical or emotional gratification. There is always something at the center of our personal world. Always.

Every person is born with a burning question in his or her soul. It is probably something like, "Why?" Questions plague us. Like:

"Why was I born? Why did grandma die? Why am I so lonely? Why does my heart hurt when I cry? Why aren't I as pretty as she? Why are there wars? --and sickness? --and death? — Why ME?" When things go wrong in our lives, we cry, "It isn't fair!" When we hurt, we search for someone to listen and to care. We want someone to "BE there" for us- to listen, to care, and perhaps to answer our questions.

In life, we look for answers that make sense to us and make us feel more secure. Eventually, each of us finds a set of principles or beliefs that explain most of our burning questions. Or, if we can't find the answers that settle most of our questions, we keep running so fast, keep acquiring new "toys," keep so busy with things and activities that we won't have to worry about any of the burning questions buried deeply within.

And if the answers we choose for ourselves don't really settle our hearts, we get older and angrier, and angrier, and sicker, and then we die.

Maybe this would be the time for you to discover the center of your life. I, for one, do not subscribe to a commonly-held parental philosophy that says, "Well, I'm not going to push my kids in any particular direction when it comes to church or God. I'm not going to tell them what to believe. I'm just going to let my children make up their own mind about religion."

Let's face it. Our children learn attitudes about politics, about families, about right and wrong, you name it, from...that's right... from their parents. And if they don't hear your words, they certainly learn what you believe by your actions. If you have no organized approach to your individual belief system -- then identify what you DO have. Find what you believe. Live it and teach it. At least, if you do that much, your kids might have a chance to find their way through the world you leave them.

I am a Christian by cultural pattern and by personal choice. As a child, I was taken to various churches by my parents and grandparents, though sometimes puzzled by the differing worship formats in different churches, I was a social person and enjoyed church activities as part of community life. I have vivid memories of our small-town church holiday celebrations (especially Christmas!) and of being taught Bible stories in Sunday School.

One of our Methodist preachers, a short round, bald older man named Reverend Hurder, with a husky, deep voice and a slight lisp, assigned one child each Sunday to bring an article next week for a children's object lesson at the beginning of the regular church service. It was a big challenge to see who might stump the pastor, as the child chosen brought a safety pin, a toy truck, some other household item or tool, useful or decorative, and the minister would somehow weave a Bible lesson from that object. I never saw him stumped for a way to bring God into our day-to-day lives.

As much as I enjoyed the church activity, God, Himself, however, was not particularly real to me, and as I grew older, I kept searching for Him. I wanted to believe in Him, but he seemed, most of the time, so distant, like a painting on a cathedral ceiling, untouchable.

I heard testimonies of faith as a young and impressionable child, and was quite amazed by the depth of faith exhibited by my paternal grandparents who had read the Bible aloud together to each other in their morning devotions for many years, and prayed, sliding out of their comfortable overstuffed rockers, to kneel on the floor like the paintings I had seen of children praying beside their beds.

One day my grandpa told me about a day, years before my dad, their only son, was born, their second little daughter died after a battle with scarlet fever. Grandpa said that as he knelt beside her bed in prayer, he saw an angel come down and take her up. My grandparents' grief at her death had been softened by a vision that only a relatively few people might have believed. But the smile on his face told me that even years later, it was a wonderful comfort to him, and it didn't really matter what anyone else saw or believed. My grandfather was probably the first person I ever met who was a sincere "fanatic," and though he didn't really explain his faith to me, I was in awe of him for it.

Many years later, I "accidentally" met a white-haired woman who had as a young woman helped my grandmother with her housework. Though this lady and I had never met, we attended the same Lutheran church in a larger city, 50 miles from where my grandparents had lived, and somehow, she recognized me. As we visited, she was able to tell me about my grandparents' personal epiphany, their spiritual awakening as young adults. She knew because she had been in their home at the precise time their relationship grew closer to God.

By the time I heard the story, I had experienced my own epiphany, and somehow, hearing about theirs from a woman I'd never known, was a most wonderful and reassuring experience, showing me that, just as I'd thought, some of those early morning prayers my grandparents had offered must have included ME! I could almost hear my grandpa praying, "Dear Lord, no matter what, please take care of our little strong-willed granddaughter."

It is true, I think, that one's concept of their own earthly father often affects our ability to visualize a heavenly one. My dad was a hard-working, solid, good, though somewhat uninvolved figure in my life, and one I sometimes, especially during those awkward adolescent years, had trouble snuggling up to. It was only in his later years that I found he and I were able to sit and communicate. So, naturally, I guess, it makes sense that it was later, as an adult, that I was able to find a REAL relationship with God.

Though, as a young married woman, I was involved in women's church activities and organizations, I was still searching for relevance and joined a Bible Study group that became increasingly important to me. The woman leading the group, Mary, was older, wiser, and an obvious prayer warrior who <u>believed</u> what she had studied, and encouraged those of us who were younger women to trust more completely in Christ to guide us through life. The example of maturity, love and faith was impressed on us, and became the basis of years of future growth.

One late night during the year following Katie's birth, after the children were safely tucked in their beds, and my husband lay sleeping peacefully beside me, I lifted my arms upward and asked in a whisper, "Jesus, I've tried it my way, and it hasn't worked. Please forgive my sins and come into my heart and be my Savior. Take over my life. If You are real, and I believe You are, be real to me. Give me whatever You want me to have. I'm Yours. Thank You." As tears rolled down my cheeks, the search for an inner peace that I could not quite explain, a search that had become more important than anything else in my life, at last was settled. That evening, quietly, I began to sense what the Bible calls "peace that passeth understanding." (Philippians 4:7 -- KJV)

The expression "to be born again" puzzles many people who are not evangelistic Christians, but it became real for me that night, as in the dark, beside a peacefully sleeping husband, with my three small children sleeping in their beds across the hallway, I became a new person, or ALMOST so!

Days and weeks passed. The Bible became increasingly relevant and important. I was thrilled with the faith and confidence I felt in the Lord. As I read and grew more and more vocal in my newly-found happiness, my husband, a lifelong churchgoer, also found himself increasingly "sold out" to the idea as expressed in Joshua

24:15: "as for me and my house, we will serve the Lord." – (KJV)

While we grew in our relationships with each other and with God, I can only imagine the probable and sometimes frustrating changes in me that those who loved me had to endure during those early years of vigorous study and growth within the framework of Christianity. Though occasions of living our faith within various bodies of fellow Christians have been often imperfect, sometimes disappointing, and occasionally hurtful, I never regretted the decision to allow God to operate in and through my life. Nor, it's safe to say, did Rod. Over the years, I grew to believe the confidence we placed in an eternal, loving, all-knowing God to provide for us, to guide us, to teach us -- all these things have been completely warranted.

"WHAT?! Oh, NO! Not religion! I thought this thing was going to be about FAMILIES! I've heard enough about a religion to last a lifetime, thank you very much, and I'm mot interested! No thanks! Not me! Can't we talk about SOMETHING that doesn't involve RELIGION?!'"

I do hear the same voice that may talk to you and in you. We've all heard it. But, just for a little while, lay aside your skeptical companion. Okay? Let me tell you what I learned and experienced. About families, priorities, and our need for God in the middle of it all. Later, you will have time to ponder and choose what you believe.

For many years, the beliefs and social rules of various church homes were firm guidelines in which we moved. As times changed and some of our "family rules" proved unproductive or even destructive, I eased in applying them to my life, and I became, according to my daughters, more "laid back" about the RULES of religion, and more in love with Jesus Christ, the Author and Finisher of our faith.

Some years ago, during a prayer time with a small group of believers, I saw a picture in my mind of people worshipping hand-in-hand in a huge circle around God's throne -- each person worshipping saw God from a unique angle. Worshippers turned to one another, saying, "Do you see what I see? Can you see the love?" ... "the light?" ... "the judgment throne" ... "the shepherd" ... etc. Each person saw the Lord from his/her unique perspective, which seemed to be what God IS. And sometimes people became unhappy with one another because each person had a different truth.

I, too, am Three

For me, much of my understanding of God revolves around my own understanding of Scripture, what we have learned from various teachings, and from the "on the job training" He seems to have given.

I believe strongly that when God said in scripture that He made man in His own image, it means that we are, like God, three parts, a trinity. A triune nature in man, like God's, includes a SOUL (the mind, personality, feelings, talents, etc.), and a BODY (our physical self) and a SPIRIT (the inner, God-shaped man).

Most of us understand the soul and the body. In fact, when we think of people we know, the very essence of that person, as we usually understand it, is the combination of their soul and body.

However, there is more. And most of the time, we ignore the third part in our pursuit of "happiness." The SPIRIT is the inner part of mankind that, according to scripture, died when Adam and Eve sinned in the Garden of Eden (Genesis 2:17 -- "for on the day that thou eatest thereof thou shalt surely die."-- KJV), leaving mankind cursed with an incomplete self. Now, you may not identify with the story in the Bible. And that's okay. It isn't required in order to see the truth of a spirit part of man.

How many times have you experienced an unnamed loneliness or a search for meaning and fulfillment? We try everything to satisfy it -- sports, organizations, marriage, more education, etc. As I grew up, I was an amateur actress, and found that most important part content on stage -- that part that says, "I belong here. I am alive. I am accepted." But it was always short-lived, because it ended with the end of each theater run. I became "ME" again, and "me" alone. And the emptiness, the deepest loneliness followed me into marriage and family and teaching.

You see, the spirit part of man is the part that communicates with God, that only God can fill. And it is the part of us that is "born again" when a person accepts Jesus Christ as Savior.

When we finally connect with God, our third part is opened up and alive to talk to and listen to our Creator. For the first time many people are able to accept the Bible verse "God so greatly loved and dearly prized the world [including ME!] that He (even) gave up His only-begotten (unique) Son, so that whosoever... [I'm one of those whosoever's!] ...believes in (trusts, clings to, relies on) Him shall not perish (come to destruction, be lost) but have eternal (everlasting) life." (John 3:16 -- Amplified Version [with my notes!])

So, Dear One, am I telling that you <u>must</u> follow the path I have chosen in order to find your religion -- your own center? No. You are standing in a different place, looking at God from YOUR time and experience.

But I <u>am</u> telling you that you should look at your God, your center. You must find your own answers in your search for questions like "Who am I?" ... "To whom do I belong?" ... "What, or whom can I trust in life?" ... "Why am I here?" And I am also telling you that you will never really find peace-of-mind, happiness, until you are comfortable with your answers. All the busy-ness, striving for success or physical comfort, all your running fast to find happiness is just more brush fires! And sometimes we get so caught up in fighting brush fires, we never save the forest. But your search for your Center, your God, is YOURS.

I suppose there are people in the world who fill their minds and bodies with such great activity going here and there that they don't struggle with these questions.

But I suggest that if people were honest, most of us do search for a fulfillment, some deep indescribable hunger. A college theater director once called that center the "spine" of a character in a play – his or her center-most truth.

We all look for answers that make sense to us and make us feel more secure. Every living person has a center, a religion. Yes, everyone.

Not everyone sees this search, or its answers exactly as I do, of course. Finding an understanding of God's plan for mankind to which my heart shouts, "YES!" makes wonderfully simple sense for me and satisfies my searching soul. Not all the answers come immediately.

However, as each new question comes along, As I continue along the path of my choosing, I am aware of a friendship with a real Jesus Christ, the Companion of my spirit, who is no longer a mere picture on a wall, a concept in a sermon, a statue in a church, or words written on a page. He has become my friend and a gentle, patient, quiet teacher with a keen sense of humor, who reveals to me life's answers only as I am willing to hear and comprehend them, one day, sometimes one moment, at a time. I feel peaceful as I continue to move, live, and listen for God's instruction and direction.

We search for COMPLETENESS. For me, that completeness came when I entrusted my life to God as manifested through the life and death of Jesus Christ. Since that day, I have believed that service to others was service to God, that He was my companion, my guide, my friend, my teacher and my true boss. In my heart, He did not rule with an iron fist, but with His own loving compassion for every aspect of me.

Is Christ essential for the creation of a good family?

Probably not.

Is the nuclear family, with father, mother and children in one secure home, the only successful pattern for raising a child?

Nope. (Sorry, Mom!)

Over the years, I have managed to be welcomed into the warmth of many good families who were not Christian. And so I know, as you do, that there are successful families in the world who are not Christ-centered. There are also young people who have been raised to become secure, independent, loving individuals who have not been raised in a traditional family. Those facts do not in any way diminish my belief in the strength of having a centered, complete family unit.

I repeat the question, "Is Christ essential for the creation of a good family?" Probably not. But He sure helps!

After several years of marriage, as our family began to grow, my husband and I determined together that we would not only TAKE our children to a church for someone else to educate them about religion, but we would, ourselves, be educated in the things of God. We decided that we would allow our own lives to be used as an example to our children, no matter what might come of it. Let's face it. Even a parent who won't admit it becomes an example for his/her children, of the very success or failure of his or her philosophy.

Rabbi Harold Kushner in *When Bad Things Happen to Good People*, said that theology, or telling people ABOUT God, is about as filling for the hungry soul as reading a menu is to hungry stomachs. And that description seems to apply here. What you TELL your children about your priorities in life is only about half as important (if THAT important!) as what you DEMONSTRATE about your priorities.

In our young family, we wanted an active, living relationship with God, which would hopefully be a satisfying life for our family. If knowing God intimately did not fulfill our spiritual needs or our children's spiritual needs, then theology (the study of religious principles) certainly wouldn't do it, either.

One has only to look at many of the children of not only churchgoers, but church leaders, to see the sometimes empty lives of children who know LOTS of theology, but haven't somehow internalized it into a personal, trusting relationship with God. Perhaps you're familiar with the old stereotype many times associated with "P.K.s" (preacher's kids). When I was a child, several of my "p.k." friends had already become masters at appearing religious, of acting appropriately on Sunday, in public, or in front of their parents, while acting "like hell" the rest of the week. There was an obvious desire to appear religious, but an equally obvious dissatisfaction with the principles they had been taught but had obviously not internalized.

Interestingly, as Rod and I moved our family from one geographic area to another of the United States, from one church body and denominational structure to another over a period of years, I was a bit surprised to meet and often counsel angry teens and young adult children and grandchildren of religious leaders from many different backgrounds. Of course, not all preachers' kids were rebellious and angry, and most of those who struggled with their own place in the circle of believers eventually matured and came around to a settled personal relationship with God.

In recent years, as my career of being a full-time mother and part-time Christian teacher/counselor gave way to full-time public education classroom teacher among many adolescents, I was interested to realize more fully than ever before, that a similar anger and rebellion can often be found in some children of teachers, administrators, civic leaders, and politicians.

What do these apparently successful educated people have in common with the ministers mentioned earlier? Perhaps one possibility is that parents had apparently worked for years on their <u>public image</u>, and somehow their children had found it inconsistent with their private lives at home. Certainly, another underlying problem could be the child's unsatisfied need for parental attention and acceptance.

As parents, the one thing that Rod and I did <u>not</u> want was to raise kids who rebelled against the very center of our lives because of any hypocrisy or lack of sincerity on our parts. We determined that we would LIVE what we believed, and what we spoke. We would openly share our lives with our children, other family members, and our friends. And they, we hoped, would reap the harvest of good seeds we planted in their lives. We decided not to hide anything from them, or from ourselves. If we were wrong in our faith or our philosophy, we were willing to allow them to see that, too.

I wish I could say that we were perfect parents, and that everything we attempted to be and do turned out well. It didn't. However, looking back from a distance of 30 or more years, I would not alter our goals, and I would never give up the moment long ago, when I gave control of my life's destination to Another, who loved me far better than I ever loved myself.

Again, I suspect that the majority of this philosophy was hammered out in my head first. Rod was busy with practical concerns, like supporting, feeding and sheltering, our large family. I was the one who spent more moments, sometimes hours, studying and communicating with wise people, including ministers who came to our kitchen table for a cup of coffee, conversation and prayer, away from the solitary pressures of their responsibilities.

In the evenings, after the kids went to bed, I shared my thoughts with my husband, who was not a talker. If there was an issue, a problem or concern, he would listen. And then he would take those thoughts, work through them, and return later, maybe the next day, with his answer. Usually we agreed. And usually, our conversations, if one-sided, were peaceful. We prided ourselves, I boasted, on never arguing in front of our children. If we disagreed, we did it privately. I later realized that stuffing growing dissension for the sake of outward peace may have become a flaw in the foundation of our marriage.

When we believe it, we LIVE it!

Jesus, while He lived on earth, had a number of friends who followed Him around for various reasons. Some of them were greedy, and some were curious. Some believed he was a godly teacher or rabbi, if not the Son of God. Later, many of these men were called his disciples, which means "disciplined ones," because they had been shaped by their association with The Master. But while Jesus walked the earth, few of them were more energetic in their commitment to Him then his disciple, Peter, whom Jesus called "The Rock."

One day, after miraculously feeding and teaching more than 5,000 people with five loaves of bread and two fish, Jesus sent his followers across the Sea of Galilee ahead of him in a boat. It is recorded in the Book of Matthew, Chapter 14, that as night fell, a wind storm arose, and Jesus came to the tossing boat, walking on the water! While he was still some distance from the boat, his followers saw the shape of a man walking towards them. Already frightened, they called, "Who are you?" Over the noise of the tossing waves, Jesus answered them, calling that it was He.

Apparently the majority of the disciples were still frightened, skeptical that what they were seeing was truly their Rabbi -- their teacher. Was this shape a ghost or a spirit? Though they had seen Jesus perform many amazing miracles, they were REASONABLE men, and what they were seeing now was a physical impossibility. Everyone knew that a man could not walk on the surface of water. That is, everyone except Peter.

Peter was perhaps the first person to believe that "With God nothing shall be impossible." (Luke 1:37 – KJV) And Jesus agreed. Peter looked at the "ghost" and called, "Lord, if it is You, command me to come to You on the water." (Matthew 14:28 – Amplified Bible) He put Jesus to the test, and he did it with his whole life.

Jesus said, "Come."

Now, here is the interesting part, I think. After hearing Jesus' voice, Peter climbed out of the boat, and began walking toward Jesus. On the water. No one recorded how many steps he took on the water before he looked around at the waves, and heard his disbelieving friends calling from the boat, "Hey, Peter! Get back in the boat! ... You can't do that! ... Come back! ... Come back to the boat ... You'll drown out there!"

Can't you just hear them? And they were right, you know. After listening to the "voice of reason," Peter began looking at his situation, at the waves rolling around him, and he became afraid. He began to use his logic and common sense, and he began to act logically. He began to sink! Naturally. What else would you expect?

However, as Peter began to feel the water rising above his ankles, what did he do? What was his response? Did he turn back to the boat, swimming madly? No. He called out to his Master, to

Jesus, still walking on the water, "Lord, save me!" What a wonderful reaction. If only we would respond as quickly in that way.

Immediately, Jesus took his hand and they walked to the boat together! Interestingly, as soon as they climbed back in the boat, the seas became calm. Many people talk about impetuous Peter losing faith and sinking until he had Jesus' hand. But the wonderful thing for me is the fact that Peter, for a short while, walked on top of a troubled sea! He WALKED. What he had done was impossible. But he DID it!

Had Peter not heard Jesus' voice clearly, and had he not climbed over the side of the boat, or had he not been the type of person who acted (sometimes impulsively, we know) on what he believed, he'd never have had the marvelous experience of doing the impossible!

That's the difference, in my opinion, of living in a RELATIONSHIP with God, as opposed to simply understanding the theological implications of any given situation. When you are friends with God, when you learn to recognize His voice, even in the middle of great distractions, when He says, "Come," and you know you can trust Him completely, you do what He invites you to do without reservation. You climb over the edge of apparent safety and you do amazing things without fear, because you trust your Master to grab your hand when you need it.

You can check out the story in The Gospels. And while you're reading, you'll read what Jesus said to those who watched this miracle from the safety of the boat: "But Jesus beheld them, and said unto them, with man this is **impossible**; but with God all things are possible." (Matthew 19: 26 - KJV)

I have a distinct memory of an early morning dream, one weekend while we were attending a church retreat in another town. Just before I awakened fully, I felt myself floating in what seemed like a small boat on a lake. It must have been anchored near a shore, because as I slept, I could hear gentle little waves lapping the shore. As I listened to the soft sound of the water, I heard a man's voice say quietly, "If you want to walk on the water, you need to get out of the boat." What a thought! I woke up excited about all the opportunities that would come my way when the Lord might call me to step out of the safety of my own little boat!

After we learned, through occasionally sloshing around in a pool or two, that we could trust God and His Word in our lives, we chose to serve Him as honestly and completely as we were able. We often flubbed up in our enthusiasm, and occasionally we had to be rescued from knee deep water we'd tried walking on. Overzealous at times, I'm sure, we probably took chances that weren't particularly wise. But we always called out to God for His hand, and it was always there.

In the more than 15 years that we worked with God as our official boss, we never, that I know of, told Him "No" when we both felt we'd been asked to do something for Him or His people. We were willing to take risks if it seemed to us together (this is an important point-- to be addressed later) that God wanted us to "get out of the boat and walk on the water."

And, perhaps the best thing about this time in our lives was that amazing things happened! Though life was not always easy or simple, because we were centered, we KNEW the center of our beliefs, and chose to live them fully in front of our children, I believe, we were marvelously (and divinely) protected from any sort of real harm, and our kids eventually became really neat grownups. They don't and probably didn't always agree with our decisions, but they were there, and saw most of the consequences.

Because we lived our lives so openly, we were occasionally the object of, at the very least, curiosity, and at the very most, ridicule. Because I occasionally became aware that I was considered a "fanatic" for Christ, I must tell you that one of my guiding principles is "Fanatics are Fabulous!"

Meet the Fabulous Fanatic

Trusting God completely, and relying on Him for provision, direction, etc., brands one a religious fanatic, you know.

"So, what's a fanatic?" you might ask. A fanatic is someone who cares more about anything than you do. If you know someone who absolutely loves playing golf, like my dear friend Rowena, who knew all about the different strokes, equipment, rules and personnel, you could logically, I would think, call that person a golf fanatic. And if it's Rowena, she delighted in the title!

Several years ago, my son David, who also comes close to deserving the title when it comes to golf, took me along to a driving range in order to teach me a few strokes. Though I wildly whopped that little ball with a valiant effort, I never caught the golfing bug, and just enjoyed watching my son's concentrated effort, and listening to his attempts to explain the proper swing.

I have never been a golf fanatic, though love to tag along and drive the golf cart! Earlier in my life, I was not even a FAMILY fanatic! (Well, that might be debated, I suppose, given my earlier confession about *Little Women*!) However, over the years, I didn't mind being considered a religious fanatic.

For myself, I never really cared much for people with little or no enthusiasm for life. Even though you might occasionally find the views of a fanatic rather difficult to live with, at least you never have trouble figuring out where they stand on the things or issues that fuel their passion. Whether it's exercise, golf, health food, politics or religion, their dedication and love for that especially meaningful something in their lives fires them to accomplish greatness in our world.

Personally, I never admired people with colorless personalities. Complacency, a "who cares?" attitude about life, seems to bring about a colorless personality, and I'd rather have a friend with a strong personality -- a colorful red, purple, orange, green, or even black personality. Bland beige or colorless gray personalities have no particular interest for me. When a person cares enough to take a definite, unwavering stand on behalf of his/her particular cause, you can depend upon that person to do or be whatever he or she says.

I, for one, admire courage and dedication, even fanaticism in a person, and I suppose I somehow encouraged that sort of single-mindedness in my children. I admire individuals. I admire commitment. And I admire colorful personalities, inner peace, and a certain amount of, okay, "fanaticism" -- especially for good causes. This is very different from the examples of fanaticism I see today expressed by militant, ugly, hate-filled, angry, violent people who DEMAND that they be acknowledged. Sad, sad, sad.

So, I'm a Christian fanatic. And I absolutely accept the label. Even treasure it. Why? Because, for one thing, God is not particularly impressed with lukewarm children.

Check out this scripture: "I know your [record of] works and what you are doing; you are neither cold nor hot. Would that you were cold or hot! So, because you are lukewarm and neither hot nor cold, I will spew you out of My mouth!" (Revelations 3:15—16, Amplified Bible) Spew, by the way, means to spit or vomit. And the speaker of the passage is God, talking to the church – believers -- us.

I would never want God to consider me lukewarm, so I chose to be hot rather than cold for God. Hot means active, living, moving, and sometimes standing out on a limb, alone. Or maybe it means climbing over the side of a boat on stormy waters.

Now, what does this have to do with children?

Perhaps this: If you follow the principles I'm sharing, you may find yourself parenting, teaching or counseling young people who develop strong personalities and strong convictions. Interestingly, your own kids may not be particularly similar to you in their interests, their personalities, or even their "fanaticisms." Your young people will hopefully have many of the same primary beliefs that you shared with them and lived in front of them as they grew. But they will express it in their own unique manner.

That, however challenging, is wonderful! Let's hear it for the fanatics! Yes!

And while we're at it, let's hear it for a decision each couple or single parent must make about the center of the family. What are you going to build upon? A dream? A quest for things? A principle of living peacefully with your fellow man? A philosophy? A religion?

Think about it. Whether you know it or not, you already have a foundation in your life. Even now. Recognize and name it. Live for it. And your children will build upon it.

What will be your center? I cannot choose for you, Dear Hearts.

"But as for me and my house, we shall serve the Lord." (Joshua 24:15 - KJV)

Okay. We've covered the serious "preachy" material. Now let's talk about raising good kids.

CHAPTER 3

Men and Women in Little Packages

What sort of adults do you enjoy most? Are you impressed with strong people? Sensitive people? How about mild-mannered, optimistic, happy people?

I rather like them all, actually!

Well, now that you've considered a few of the different types of adults with whom you'd enjoy sharing your life, I'd like you to consider this little proverb from the poem "My Heart Leaps Up," written by William Wordsworth in 1802:

"The child is the father of the man."

As you deal with children, their first steps, their temper tantrums and their first attempts at independence, consider that inside this bitty body and childish personality lives a grown man or woman.

Every gift or talent, and every strength he or she will ever possess is already there. These wonderful qualities are perhaps not channeled or developed yet. But they're all there. Remember our little discussion about the spirit part that asks, "Who am I?" The spirit, whom only God can fulfill, is part of the human package at birth. We have baby bodies to take care of, and childish minds to train. But the soul of a man or woman lives in the body of a tiny child.

A new life is like a package, a gift, we often say, that has been carefully wrapped by God, given to parents to protect and unfold with the passage of time. And the new life comes complete with numerous wonderful qualities inside, waiting to be discovered, channeled and strengthened. Helping our children grow up is like unwrapping each portion of the package, and each portion is particularly important.

It is also very important that as we parents expose each part of those gifts and talents to our children, we are careful about what we emphasize. Do we point out our children's good qualities, their important uniqueness, and the wonder of their individuality? Or do we point out their personality weaknesses, their repeating of "dumb mistakes," or their bad habits?

I believe with all my heart that it is the job of the parent to notice the GOOD things about the "man" (or "woman") who lives within the child. How does that translate into our everyday relationship with our kids? It means that we as parents, teachers and counselors have to respect the child whose behavior is less than perfect. We must respect him or her enough to believe that he wants to behave well.

Sometimes we say, "I love you enough to know that you want to grow into a fine man, and this behavior is not acceptable."

Or...

"I don't like what you are doing. And I need to punish your behavior. But I love you."

Or...

"You are a wonderful person. I will always love you. I don't like what you are doing right now. But that doesn't change the fact that I love you."

Of course, we don't always use all these words, but our <u>actions</u> will either say something like this, or will give a totally different message indeed. It IS possible to discipline and correct behavior in a child without destroying the grownup inside.

Probably the worst message we could give a child would be "If you don't behave the way I expect you to behave, I will not love you." And parents say that, too, in many wordless ways.

Sometimes parents seem to get the idea we were appointed the judge of our kids' intrinsic value. And these judgments are based not on the very unique package they carry in their spirit and soul, their inner man, but on their daily childish behavior.

Does this sound familiar?

"Little Timmy is such a bad little kid -- always tearing around. He never listens to instructions. And yesterday he bit his sister. He'll never amount to anything."

Parents, grandparents, aunts and uncles, and even the neighbors, move from one level of judgment to another. And eventually, we forecast what sort of future our children will have.

Sadly, the negative predictions or prophecies also often come true. Remember hearing, "He's just like that no-good Uncle Tony." … Or… If you don't watch out, you're going to just grow up to be fat and lazy if you don't start picking up after yourself!"… and there's always … "She has the WORST hair! She'll never be able to do anything with it!"

Parents must, and I do repeat MUST, believe with all their hearts that their young, small, sometimes unruly person, is absolutely priceless to God, and therefore to us. And we parents need to be very cognizant of our children's wonderful value, even when they misbehave.

Another kind of prophecy we parents get caught up in is when we say that a certain age in the growing process is going to be "terrible" for us. It may be the "two's" or it may be the teen years. We have ample opportunity to decide with the written materials available to us, that certain phases of childrearing are more difficult for many people than others. And of course, even before we get to that particular stage, we all feel fairly inadequate when we realize the awesome responsibility parents have.

I remember hearing so much about "the generation gap" years ago, and wondering while my own children were younger, if it would be as tough to raise teenagers as everyone seemed to say it was. And over the years of secondary school teaching, I've certainly seen a large share of angry, rebellious and troubled teens. The adolescent years, like any other period, have their unique and important challenges. But believe me when I tell you that <u>it is not a hopeless time</u>.

After nearly 25 years of working with adolescents, I find that the needs and wishes of young people really haven't changed all that much. Young people still hope for a happy future, and they need someone who believes in their intrinsic value. Some of them have not learned that progress usually requires effort, and some of them believe that they have more rights than responsibility. However, underneath it all, they want to know the truth, and will eventually be thankful that you gave it to them.

Many times during the busy years of child rearing, I threw my tired body on my bed and repeated to myself, "This, too, shall pass" which meant "Hang in there! Everything is transitory!" Or, like someone with a wry sense of humor said while removing a child's sliver, "It'll feel better when it quits hurting!"

In order to "train up a child in the way he should go," (Proverbs 22:6 - KJV) parenting is an arduous task that takes courage, hope, humor, faith, and every bit of the concentrated energy you have to give.

And it's true. About as soon as you have passed through one particularly exciting or challenging moment in life, you're smack dab in the middle of another one and don't even know how you got there!

Parents who trust in God find each stage of child development a certain challenge, and filled with its own rewards. Believe me, when the going gets tough, "this too shall pass" helps. Interestingly, occasionally, when we move into the next level of development, we may wish we had the challenges we bemoaned last week! There are scriptures that apply here, too, about the Lord giving us the strength for the task of today, and encouraging us not to worry, but to trust the Lord in ALL matters. Try II Corinthians 12:9 and Matthew 6: 33-34 for starters. Check it out.

And while you're looking for Bible verses to hold near your heart during your parental journey, here are a couple of sweet praises from the Book of Psalms, King James Version:

"I will love Thee, O Lord, my strength." (Ps 18:1)

"It is God that girded me with strength, and maketh my way perfect. (Ps 18:3-33)

CHAPTER 4

"It Usually Takes Two"

"In the beginning," there were two people who loved each other, or at least THOUGHT they loved each other. And out of that love for each other, they created a child. Commitment -- Marriage -- Children.

The normal progression of a love relationship between a man and a woman usually includes these three steps. I repeat, "NORMAL,' though I might better have chosen the word "traditional." Today the middle step, marriage, seems to have been replaced by more "modern" arrangements in the lives of many people. And, of course the order of these three steps might be arranged in several different manners.

Perhaps I am from a different era, (and **that** is certainly true!) but don't statistics suggest that couples who experiment with an almost-committed living arrangement more often than not later experience predictable problems in their marriage? Seems so. Am I not also correct in saying that the Bible talks about a marriage of a man and a woman defining "marriage?" Seems so. For generation following generation, families are the natural order of things, particularly within a framework called "marriage." I believe boys and girls learn their parenting skills by remembering their childhood. Studying and learning about a family from reading books is a good thing. Living within a good, loving family is even better.

Growing up, every young girl I ever knew dreamed of one day marrying the man of her dreams. Though statistics today indicate that marriages are in trouble, at the vast majority of wedding ceremonies, families congratulate the newly-weds with the highest hopes for their happiness and the longevity of their wedded bliss. Most people seem to have positive feelings about marriage in spite of some of the more disheartening current statistics. I, for one, believe in the institution wholeheartedly. Marriage CAN be wonderful, though you and I both know full well that it often is not.

Not every family begins with the perhaps oversimplified pattern of commitment -- marriage -- children, but in whatever order they may occur, these three elements are very important.

As soon as two people have committed themselves to a life together, they have begun a family. What is your idea of "family?" Certainly, it will reflect what you have experienced or read. Perhaps a mother and a father sharing a home with several children seems "right" to you. Perhaps not.

Here is a question to answer for yourself. How essential are both a mother and a father to the success of a family? Perhaps at the onset, it would be good for a young couple to agree on that very thing.

You say to yourself, "Okay. We will stay married as long as it seems to be working. On the other hand, if we begin to feel that things don't seem to be working out between us, or perhaps someone more in tune with my ideas, or more attractive to my eye comes along, we will just divorce with no hard feelings!"

Today, many couples of all ages face the fact that divorce,

easy to accomplish, is perhaps the quickest way to settle marriage difficulties. And today, because of separation or divorce, many young children grow up in a single parent home. You, as an adult, need to decide if you are going to jump the marriage ship when the seas of matrimony become stormy or boring, or if you are going to "batten down the hatches" and stay with marriage even if you aren't living "happily ever after."

About a day, perhaps a week, month, or three years after the wedding, you begin to realize that all the wonderful excitement you once felt while first doing the laundry together, the thrill of planning and cooking dinner together every day, changing the bedding, picking up another person's dirty socks and underwear, and trying to agree on the best way to spend "our" money, (ouch!) somewhere along the way stopped being wonderful, and became BORING and somewhat MONOTONOUS. Waking up to the same disheveled face on the pillow beside you, and early morning kisses laced with the same old bad breath, has somehow seriously damaged much of the blush of early romance.

Perhaps a month or year, or even <u>ten</u> years after you say, "I do," you begin to wonder why you did! Unfortunately, sooner or later, most marriages become less a matter of following one's feelings, and more a matter of honoring one's commitments. And honoring commitments or promises isn't always doing what we FEEL like doing. And it isn't always looking for the easiest or the quickest solutions to the problems between us.

I grew up waiting for a Prince Charming to come rescue me from what turned out to be a prison of pretty much my own construction. Dreams about growing up, falling in love and belonging with a man who loved me, really loved who I was, not just how I looked or what I said, had filled my adolescence. I do not know how I can describe myself as a young person, other than to say I was filled with passion, idealism and creativity, and had virtually no idea how to live with these inner churnings. So alone. So hungry for love and acceptance and "normalcy."

And then, one day, there I was, sitting at my mother's kitchen table, sewing for my last semester of college, and having coffee with mom, Ola, a carpenter who was adding a room to our house, and his son, a lovely young man who had just arrived home from the stress of early Viet Nam. He, Rodney, said little, smiled shyly and listened to me as if I were the most enchanting girl he'd ever known, and he obviously had not known many girls! That night, I eventually learned, he told two of his best friends that he'd met the girl he was going to marry. Though I only dreamed it, Rod had decided that we were going to be a couple.

They say that opposites attract, and I suppose it is true. I finally felt that maybe I could live a normal life with a "real" person. Ours was a quick courtship, lasting 3 months and 3 days!. We were both very happy in many ways. Rod and I had, nearly from day one, rather different personalities, much like Mutt and Jeff, salt and pepper, or lightening and picnics in the park! Our great differences were for years the strengthening as well as the challenge of our marriage.

My husband was by both nature and habit, and progressively, as years went along, more and more by his own conscious choice, I think, a silent and private man. I, always the idealist and probably eternally naive, endowed him with inner qualities that he never had, and probably never really wanted. The inner strength and wisdom I attributed to him in his silence eventually began to crumble the more I leaned on it, and the longer we lived together.

Before too many years, we both found ourselves living separate internal lives. Because our core beliefs were the same, our life goals similar, and we were basically nice people, most observers thought we were a great pair. But that's only part of the story. Talk about oil and water mixing! Takes a whole lot of shaking! We had not been married long before I knew that the differences between us would be tough ones to live with. Rod enjoyed being married to me as long as I didn't nag him to "share." I most appreciated being married to him when I could feel his friendship and protection as well as his ardor.

I remember the first time I "got" that our marriage was in serious jeopardy because of our different expectations. We'd been married about three years and I had become increasingly dissatisfied with the level of our communication. When we began having children, we agreed that I should quit teaching and stay home with them. I still think it's the best decision if one has the choice, and my hard-working husband gave me that option. I'll always be glad for that.

So, I had two beautiful babies at home, and a husband who came home from work each night with very little to talk with me about. I found that I NEEDED to talk to an adult after a day of runny noses, potty training, cooking, cleaning and laundry that became mountainous tasks. Oh, how I hung on each word about his work and the world outside my little house. I poured out each detail about our days. We'd eat, watch a little television, play with and bathe the children, and then go to bed. Usually, he'd drop right off to sleep while I'd have to read for awhile in order to get to sleep. Sometimes, surrounded by those I loved, I ached with a familiar but disquieting loneliness. Sound familiar?

Well, one night, in bed, before my innocent husband fell asleep, I decided to share my heart and soul as completely as I knew now, telling Rod that I felt a most serious need for the things I believed most women needed in a man -- talking, especially. I told him I wanted us to be real soul mates. Once that door was opened, and he looked me in the eyes, I continued on, telling him about my passion for theatre and teaching, for reading, and conversation, and travel, and the need I had for a real friendship between us. I ached from all that I wanted him to understand about me -- my hopes and dreams, my desire for a deeper love with him. Oh, such things I shared!

My young husband, whom I so desperately wanted to love me in the most complete fashion I could dream, lay beside me in bed as I began to unload the burden in my heart, hands clasped behind his head, looking much of the time at the ceiling while I talked, cried, blew my nose, and kept on talking.

And at the appointed time, when I'd run out of words, when I'd poured out every need and desire that I could think of, I saw in the silence, a look akin to panic cross his eyes as he glanced uncomfortably at me. He knew I'd run down. He knew it was his turn. He swallowed, took a deep breath or two, and said, "What do you mean?"

That was the moment I knew the kind of communication I had always thought possible, had always longed for in a mate, was very likely not going to be a part of my marriage. And I knew that any future long "unburdening sessions" on my part would very likely chase him further away from me. I realized that I must quit trying to force him to trust me enough to talk, REALLY talk with me.

What to do? Remember now, in the calendar of events, this one-sided conversation took place a couple of years earlier than my moment of surrender to Jesus. I had not given my heart fully to the Lord, though I wore the label and certainly acted the part with sincerity. It was a little later that a relationship with Jesus became real in my heart.

Had we followed the urgency of my damaged emotions and dreams immediately after that night, we could have dissolved our marriage, and just given up. In some respects, I suppose, it might have been easier. Our children were very young, and we were, too. Both of us believed very strongly in the importance of marriage, of a complete family unit within which kids could grow strong.

And we both wanted to love each other. I have absolutely no doubt about that.

Following that evening, after years of exercise, I learned to be a little more patient, perhaps, and rather less demanding of that treasured communication. Over a period of time, we chose to work together with as much harmony as possible, to live peacefully, and respectfully. And for a good number of years, we were quite successful. Both of us believed in the strength of working as a united team.

Without talking all of our differences through as thoroughly as we might have, we chose to respect each other and the uniqueness of our individual personalities. And sometimes we chose to love each other and work together in spite of our feelings. You will notice that I have used the word "we." But, to tell you the truth, "we" never discussed it much. I think the fact that neither one of us was willing to "talk it through," that both of us wanted peace between us at nearly any price, was the small crack in our foundation that eventually caused it to crumble. Had I to do it over today, I think I'd have forced us to talk. Not fight, but talk, until there was a real resolution. How wise is hindsight.

At any rate, we chose to love in spite of our feelings. For, you see, I believe that most of the time love is a choice. How can you stay married when your feelings are occasionally hurt, or you sometimes feel unloved or angry, or disappointed, or just plain bored? How can you stay married when you lose the sense of self worth that seemed to be a part of those first months of being in love?

How did we do it for so many years? Simply put, we CHOSE to. Over the years following that fateful conversation, I learned that my mind or my will is stronger than my feelings and emotions. Emotions flare up more quickly, and sometimes they are loud and very strong, for a while. However, they are not often very reliable witnesses. And emotions fade and change.

Consider the report that two individuals might give you of the same episode. One child, Billy, slams through his mother's kitchen door crying, "Mom! Look! I got a black eye because Jimmy hit me in the eye with his bat. He hates me! And I hate him!" Trying not to scream or faint, mother takes care with needed first aid and rushes out to confront Jimmy, the little monster!

Jimmy, the little coward, ran home because he knew he was in serious jeopardy of, at the very least, a good tongue lashing. Billy's mother is prepared to follow the demon to the ends of the earth to make him pay. She is being led by her strong emotions.

Meanwhile, as she's crossing the baseball park to get to Jimmy's house, the Little League coach meets her on the sidewalk, and worriedly asks, "How's Billy?" As she starts to describe his injury, he puts his arm around mother, who is obviously upset, leads her over to a nearby bench, and several other parents follow. All of them begin sympathetically relaying details of the "accident."

Interestingly, Jimmy, the cowardly little devil, appeared to have hit little Billy because Billy is a klutz and walked into the bat while Jimmy was practicing his swing behind the plate. The so-called "neutral observers," not affected by their emotional response to the incident, explain to Billie's mom that Jimmy, blinded by the sunlight, and Billy, yelling taunts at the opposing team, had accidentally collided, though the fans seemed to hint at a slightly different interpretation as to who was the potential monster! It seems that Jimmy now has a loose front tooth from Billy's angry punches following the incident! Sometimes being a mother and learning the truth about your children can be quite a shocking experience, particularly when our initial emotional reaction is proven an overstatement.

Truth, for the most part, cannot be accurately observed and interpreted by emotion. I have come to realize it more strongly with every passing year. I can't tell you the number of times when an initial emotional response to any situation would have led to unhappy consequences for teachers, administrators, students and parents.

Most certainly, the same is true within family units. Though I might initially FEEL otherwise, when I decide to act within the boundaries of love and patience towards someone, amazingly quickly, my emotions line up with the decision I've made. It may take a few minutes, sometimes hours or days, but feelings are very changeable and flexible. Angry, sad or lonely feelings and emotions need to be fed and encouraged in order to grow. It seems to me that our decisions are stronger than our emotions, and we can choose what we pay most attention to and feed -- good feelings or bad ones.

Try this sometime: One morning in front of your mirror, you decide, "This is going to be a good day. I love my life. Everyone likes me. And I am basically a happy person." Some individuals repeat these or similar phrases aloud as a mantra, each morning, in order to establish their thought patterns for the new day.

Check later in the day. How did your day go? Usually pretty well, if you set your mind on the right path, in spite of life's unexpected twists and turns.

You know, don't you, that the opposite is also possible. There are days for each of us when we decide, usually basing our decision for the day on some impression or feeling when we first get out of bed, that this day is going to be a tough one. And it usually is, isn't it? You may feel depressed, but it's only what you <u>decide</u> about those feelings, and what <u>weight</u> you choose to give them each day that determine their importance in your daily life.

Anyone who knows me knows that I'm not really an early morning person. I don't enjoy getting up before sunrise. And occasionally, getting up in the dark can affect my attitude about a day. I believe it's true that I usually have the kind of day I've decided to have. On the early mornings when I SAY to myself, "I love teaching. I love those teenagers, and it thrills me to see them grow," my feelings agree. Knowing the students I will see each day, I find it helps me when I pray for the Lord to bless them and me, too, as I prepare for the day's work. Amazingly, the sun comes, I smile at myself in the mirror before I leave the house, and the world around me seems to agree, "This is an okay day."

How does it work? Is it self-hypnosis? Not at all. Mind control? Nope. I just put my will in a more powerful position in my life then my feelings. I have found that what I believe in my heart, and speak, even to myself in my mind, will be true in my emotions.

People tell me that I'm a loving person, and I guess it's true. However, I love people because somewhere along the way, I CHOSE to love them. Jesus spoke often about love being the natural response of a heart that is right with God, and I have found that as I get older and submit more of my life to Him, His responses become more and more natural within me.

You don't always have to make conscious decisions each moment of the day. Eventually, loving becomes a natural response. But to begin with, before my automatic response to people was a loving acceptance, I just decided to love them. And, you know what?! It worked!

I love you because I choose to love you. I forgive you because I choose to forgive you. I have peace in my life because I choose to be peaceful, and to pursue peace in my relationships.

Back to love and the family!

Okay, so we've decided to love. Now, what, exactly, IS love? Think about it. Many people say to one another, "I love you," but then act like enemies to one another. Which speaks louder to other people, our words or our actions? Words?! Hey! Give me a break!

Actions speak more profoundly, of course!

I remember being told by a person years ago that he loved me, that I was special and wonderful. Then, whenever we were in public, he proceeded to act like I was invisible. Words have always been important to me, and so, for a time, I believed him. However, eventually I realized that his words didn't mean much because his behavior told me emphatically that I was not particularly important to him. After a time of struggling to align his private words and my experience with his public action, trying to feel loved, but instead, beginning to doubt myself worthy of anything real, I, eventually no longer listened to his sweet words, or cared to try. Our relationship ended "not with a bang," but in silence. I suspect both of us were disappointed.

The same type of thing is possible within the family. We may send cards and gifts with sweet notes almost dripping with sentiment on birthdays and holidays like Christmas or Valentines Day. And those things are very nice. However, if we act carelessly or disrespectfully toward our loved ones the rest of the year, don't you think individual family members might justifiably question the depth of our love for them? Loving someone is certainly more than words. Love is also action. Action says, "You are important to me. You are a valuable part of my life. I have told you. Now let me show you."

How do we show that we love each other? As parents and as children, as well as friends, we are very able to show our love for one another by choosing to treat each other with respect.

If you had a precious, even priceless piece of art -- a painting or sculpture -- that had been given to you, you wouldn't ignore it. You might even keep it in a secret place, and you would not THINK of leaving it unguarded in the middle of a public place where it could be stolen or damaged. Because you are a reasonable person, one who chooses to value the really valuable things in your life, you would guard and protect a precious treasure.

Love, perhaps our most precious treasure in life, must be guarded and protected, too. A person who means a great deal to you is worth watching over, protecting from neglect, abuse or theft. <u>Spend time</u> (perhaps, in this rapidly moving world, our most important commodity) <u>nurturing that which is precious to you.</u> And I'm not talking about sitting together in front of the same television program! TELL your loved ones that you value them, and then show them by giving them your time, and your attention.

In a special treasure chest in my bedroom, I have a collection of love notes and art work from my children, written on special occasions and on "regular" days, too.

I also have precious memories of hugs and kisses during my days with my children, of little souvenirs from their field trips and vacations. I remember the year Andrew was ten and spent three weeks of summer vacation with his Aunt LaVonne 500 miles from home. When he returned home, his proudest moment came in presenting me with a dozen juice glasses he had purchased with his very own lawn mowing money at a garage sale! He said, "I knew you needed them, Mom!" He was right. I did need them. And I LOVED it that he had thought of me when he had money in his hand. At that moment I was absolutely certain that, no matter how far apart we were geographically, I was loved!

My children were able to show me their love in many ways as they matured. They cleaned their room when I asked, or washed dishes or mowed the lawn. Sometimes they telephoned me when they knew they'd be late returning home from a date. I tried to show them, however busy I might be, that each of their stories was important to me, and each of their requests demanded a loving, (<u>not</u> fake or mushy!) courteous response. Just as I expected courtesy in their responses to me and each other, even when we disagreed, my conversation or instruction to them should never be laced with sarcasm.

As my children matured, and spent more time away from home, I developed the habit of waking just about the time they got home from a late night. I always asked them to tell me they were home, even if they thought I was asleep. I have two distinct memories of those late nights. Kathy, always wishing not to disturb me, would tiptoe into our bedroom and stand quietly beside me as I slept, probably for a minute or two, until I became aware of her, and woke on my own so she could tell me she was home safe, and get a goodnight hug. Sometimes it was rather startling to wake suddenly and find her standing there, but now it's a sweet memory to me.

Another of my favorite memories involved Kevin and his good friend Amos, who lived with us during their senior year in high school, after his parents had been transferred to New Orleans. Amos wanted to graduate with his friends, so for a year, we were his "almost" parents. Randy and John were married and on their own by this time, and Kevin and Amos had a fun year together. Coming home from a senior activity late at night, to a darkened house, I remember the two boys silhouetted in the doorway of our bedroom, recounting the events of the night. The quiet talking and laughing often lasted for quite a long time before they went on to bed, and Rod and I could settle down to sleep, confident that everyone was home safe.

Thoughtfulness and courtesy, no matter what the circumstances, don't come naturally. People have to be taught that kindness and concern for the other person is also important in keeping any relationship in tact.

Teaching and modeling these things are important parts of parenting. Maybe the most important things if we want our kids to grow up with these values.

Back to marriage. In those stressful moments when negative emotions may be trying to separate two people who are committed to each other, perhaps married couples need to decide why they got married in the first place. Getting married in order to satisfy family, legal or society's moral standards in order to protect a sexual relationship is not a sufficient basis for marriage.

Marriage, in my opinion, is a commitment to one another, a binding commitment to continue a relationship even after some of the initial romantic passions have subsided. I think we Americans have become, perhaps, too accustomed to quick cereals, life wrapped in protective plastic, and quick answers to our problems. We want to live on promises based on good intention, but little commitment.

As a teenager during the late fifties and early sixties, my preparation for marriage was quite dependent upon romantic novels, music by Johnny Mathis, and innocent television programs like *The Brady Bunch, I Love Lucy* and *Life with Father*. I sincerely believed that a "good" marriage was one created around a romance, and could, over the years, thrive on continued romance between partners. What a shock it was to realize a few years later, that romance, along with memories of moonlight and roses preserved between pages of an old book, had faded and lost its freshness, and marriage roles were not as clearly and idealistically defined as I'd always hoped.

In absolute desperation, I found myself reading every secular and Christian counseling book about marriage and the family that I could get in my hands. Some of them were good, and a couple of the books and manuals were quite wonderful. In fact, the owner of a local Christian book store began channeling new books my way, knowing I was one of his best publicists!

Still, it eventually came down to our own family finding the manner in which we could live and work together in the peace, harmony and love that the Bible talked about.

During that time of intense study, I read in some well-meaning Christian materials that I as a wife was to portray (much like acting or pretending, if it didn't come from the heart) a certain wifely role in order to get my husband and children to conform to a perfect Biblical pattern. If I remember correctly, that was the week I ran out and bought a house dress, sensible shoes and an apron, and met Rod at the door with a plate of freshly baked cookies! As I recall, the dress made it through one washing. The cookies were finished before dinner.

I read about prayer, and went to numerous workshops and Christian retreats. Some were quite wonderful. But I wasn't always sure that I was praying right, especially if my prayers weren't answered exactly as I'd envisioned. I continued to ask God to change things… but usually not me!

I also studied about submission, which, at that time seemed to be quite a major teaching emphasis among some of our ministers. (Probably somewhat in response to the rather militant Women's Movement activities of that time.) Following the traditions of the orthodox Jewish worship patterns, women were to "keep silent" in and out of the church, in order for the men to come into their proper place as a spiritual head of the home, a leader for wife and children.

As a person who was particularly interested in love and communication, much of my personal search concerned the frustrating job of trying to mold and bend my own personality into an image of the "perfect" woman I studied in Proverbs 31. I even remember driving my car one afternoon and praying "Oh Lord, I try and try so hard to be what you seem to want me to be. But I just can't seem to get it right. What's wrong with me? If you wanted all this, how come you made me the way I am?!"

Did you ever see the cute little puppet on *Sesame Street* who, while trying to compose "Row, row, row your...balloon..." kept banging his head on the keyboard because he couldn't find "boat," and saying in utter despair, "I'll never get it! I'll never get it!"

Sometimes that's about how I felt! Everything seemed so simple on the pages. And oh, how I read! It seemed if I could just make myself better, BE better, do all I could do, then all the imperfections in life and my relationships would smooth out!

Each of the books about relationships, family, prayer, and women had certain elements of truth in them. Sometimes, today, looking back at that time, I wonder if perhaps I tried to follow too many over-simplified formulas, however well-intentioned they may have been.

Ultimately, like the scriptures say about each person working out his or her own salvation (Philippians 2:12), each marriage must also work out the unique commitment that the partners can live with together.

Once more, it takes a <u>decision</u> to live and work together peacefully, especially if the passion and awed tenderness of early romance has dwindled. I did not always understand the word "commitment," or the part that decisions and choices play in successful marriages and family. My ideas about marriage and family were rather a smorgasbord of my early expectations and dreams and all the books I tried to assimilate.

It was in India some years ago that I first saw the results of marriages built with no apology, on commitment rather than romance. In India, the majority of marriages were arranged by parents for their children. Even most Christian marriages are negotiated by families matching partners -- the more loving parents seek their children's consent, of course. As I traveled in India, I wondered if the people were happy, if the children were content and well raised.

True, from an American viewpoint, there were observable problems within some Indian homes. For one, much like Indian social structure, the family roles were so clearly defined that even upper class women sometimes functioned as little more than servants in their own homes.

However, when one looks at the family structure in societies with arranged marriages, it seems that the expectations of one marriage partner on the other are more clearly defined, and perhaps more easily satisfied than the American "happily ever after" expectation. Children in those societies know that their homes are secure, as divorce is extremely rare, almost unheard of, and certainly a cause for family shame within the community. Parents are committed to their children, to their family unit, and usually would not think of placing their family's pride in the middle of the scandal that a divorce would bring.

I'm not saying the system is perfect. And there are horrid stories of abuse. It just seems bad people everywhere do bad things. Good people (or people seeking "good") do good things. In India, I saw husbands and wives who basically came into their marriages as virtual strangers, later enjoying one another's company, planning together, cooperating, treating each other with esteem and love, and raising polite, happy and obviously secure, affectionate children.

Some few years ago, I remember precious time spent with a Pakistanian Christian pastor who had brought his beautiful wife and large family to America for a few years. During one of our many shared meals together as families, as they told the story of their arranged marriage, I was astounded that they had not spent much time together until their wedding day. William and Miriam obviously loved each other, though they said they had not known each other well at the time of their wedding. The romance that we base so much of our married lives upon had not become part of their lives until AFTER their commitment to one another. They were such basically good people whose respect, concern and, yes, love, for one another was obvious.

This couple were our good friends, and their children were very secure, very loving -- even with each other -- and refreshingly normal. At that time their oldest two children were 14 and 12-year-old daughters. Marriage was some time away, but I was curious, and so I asked them who would choose their daughters' marriage partners. William and Miriam expected their marriages to be arranged, even if they continued to reside in the United States. Would it be parents or children? And William answered, "I will decide, of course. My children have learned to trust my decisions. When they were small, I chose the shoes they wore, choosing which were best for them. Who else knows them better then their mother and I? Who loves them more? Certainly, it is my responsibility to choose their husbands."

You know, when I thought about the love and trusting relationships I had witnessed in their family, the idea of parents being involved in the selection of marriage partners for their children didn't seem particularly unreasonable to me at all.

Don't panic. I'm not suggesting a cultural revolution. I promise. I was just impressed by the neat, trusting relationship witnessed in this family.

What a different response we American parents would receive from our youngsters if we would DARE to suggest an appropriate mate. Why, I remember that I dated a few boys in high school and college simply because my parents let me know that they didn't think my choices particularly wise. My theme song for a period of time was, "Please, Mom and Dad, let me make my own mistakes!" They did. And I did. Surely, there would have been a better way then to rather blindly follow my emotions and glands, looking for the love and security I so desperately wanted.

I am not by any imaginative stretch, saying that Americans

should return to a method of selecting a mate that we long ago left behind. However, perhaps it would not harm us to consider some of the benefits, some of the reason and courtesy often more evident in other cultures.

As an observer of people for a certain number of years, I have begun to catalogue a few basic ideas about men and women. See what you think.

First, **men and women, for the most part, often marry for different reasons.** Does that seem shocking? Well, perhaps it is. Oh, both men and women usually fall in love. But it seems to me that at least until recent years, many women married in order to complete themselves. That seems to be because many women take their identity from the RELATIONSHIPS they have.

If you ask a group of women, "Who are you?" they will often answer with descriptions about whose wife they are, whose mother, whose daughter, whose lover or friend, the group they belong to, etc. If I as a woman don't know who I am, or to which group I belong, I will tell you who others say that I am, or what others say about me.

Men, on the other hand, seem to have a more FUNCTIONAL understanding of themselves, and of their marriages. If you ask a man who he is, he will often tell you about what he does. His identity depends on his job or his skills. "I'm a carpenter, I enjoy building model trains, and I jog three miles each day." Many (though certainly not all) men seem to distrust deep emotional relationships with women, and may tend to disguise rather then admit their true feelings in talking to women.

For men, marriage means living together, <u>doing</u> together. Women want <u>being</u> together. And there IS a difference. Interestingly, if you ask a man about his marriage, he will often describe the success or failure of his marriage in terms of how the partners function together, while his wife will tell you about their relationship, their communication, etc.

What a challenge it is for married couples to really understand their own needs, as well as the needs of their mates, and further, to bend their selfish desires for their own needs to be met, and to emphasize the needs important to the mate.

Well, if a good marriage is such a challenge to achieve and maintain, if it seems nearly impossible at the onset, why bother? Because, for one thing, a good marriage IS possible. It isn't automatic, but it is possible.

And a good marriage is worth it.

What is a good marriage? Certainly each person has his or her own concept of a good marriage. And you as individuals or as a couple must find your own definition -- your own goals in marriage. Since I have your attention, I will share some of what I believe possible in a good marriage. First, I believe that married people can really love (cherish and esteem) one another for a lifetime. Love changes, of course, with the seasons of life, but it can grow. Notice I said love CAN get better with age. It is not automatic. Change is not automatically improvement. Making the quality of love improve with time takes work and careful tending, like good grapes in a vineyard.

Besides the love mentioned before, a good marriage is a peaceful relationship in the middle of many stormy moments. Years ago, Rod and I decided that we would treat each other with respect, that we would not fight and that if we disagreed, we would not do it in front of our children -- at least not loudly or rudely, and NEVER violently. I must say that the number of arguments we had with one another were minimal, though there were times when we would have been better advised to have "duked it out" over an issue in order to resolve it.

Some of our inner issues were never really resolved, unfortunately.

However, one of our primary goals was to maintain a peaceful environment within our home -- a place where our kids and others could live in peaceful encouragement.

We also chose to have as the center of our home, a trust in God, as demonstrated by Jesus Christ. With that goal in mind, we found ourselves often studying Bible principles of parenting, and seeking to incorporate them into our lives.

We tried to improve ourselves, too -- a lifelong process, which our kids were allowed to observe. Rod and I were aware that young people are rather quick to discern hypocrisy, and we consciously attempted to live what we believed -- tried to "be a ... doer of the Word and not a hearer only." (James 1:23-25)

As the years progressed, it became increasingly obvious to me that marriages and families are primarily works in progress, living works of art, constantly being formed and worked on by the Master Sculptor, if He's given the chance to "sculpt," but molded by our individual decisions and the forces of life itself, if God's left out of it.

Many of our plans, and a number of our dreams changed over the years. There were detours and faltering steps along the way. Sometimes the main thing was just to keep on going. Though imperfect, if there was any sort of success in our lives together, then it was certainly worth every effort.

There are rewards in a good marriage. Two people living together in peace for a long life would seem to be a major reward in itself. Certainly, enjoying the trip together would be a major bonus. And there are the rewards of raising kids together. Sometimes it's the most bonding part of the whole experience.

CHAPTER 5

Guidelines Gathered Along the Way

Let's talk for awhile about raising good kids. So you want to have great kids?! Who doesn't?! Every mother and father who ever brought their baby home from the hospital, or adopted a child, did so with sincere hope for a wonderful future together. It's part of our human nature to look at our children and dream good dreams for them. Our kids are the hope we have that there is a happy ending, after all! And we are each determined as parents to help them find that happy ending that we may have missed for ourselves in one way or another.

Being "Mom" to nine "forever" kids gave me a certain set of, until now, "unofficial" guidelines for raising good kids. For the most part these guidelines came as a result of my own experience or study, or occasionally from observing other successful and sometimes unsuccessful families. Of course, there are no absolutes in working with flesh and blood people. Even rules carved in stone tablets may be bent at least a bit to accommodate individual families and individual needs.

The first principle for a successful family, relationship, or ANYTHING in life, was to have faith in something, and to KNOW the center of your life. **Label what you absolutely believe in and don't be wish-washy about it.**

Secondly, families need to **build on the love or commitment between two people.** Understand that there are different levels and types of love, and that love changes in its expression over the years. Anything is possible, and unlike the youth who are led around by their feelings, we have **DECIDED** to love, and to **act in a loving and respectful manner toward one another** whether we are marriage partners, parents and children, extended family members, or guests. Read I Corinthians Chapter 13 if you wonder how love acts.

A third guideline might be to **establish an underlying goal for your household.** Think about it. Can you remember a time you first entered someone's home, having a distinct impression about the people who lived there? Sometimes, before we have spent a few minutes in a family room, we have a FEELING about the general atmosphere within the family unit itself. Several distinct examples come to mind.

I remember one really neat Christian family who had purchased an older house in our hometown. They remodeled it into a beautiful home. Or their idea of a home. They had at the time, two young children and a schnauzer. After much work, the interior of the home was lovely; the colors, textures and furnishings tastefully and comfortably arranged throughout looked like beautiful, clutter-free rooms you would see in fashion magazines.

But, even more than the beautiful decor, I remember that much of the house was off limits to their children and the dog. The beautiful living room, saved for those formal occasions when important people arrived, could just as easily have been roped off like a museum display. I don't believe I, one of their very dear friends, ever sat comfortably in that room, and my children never even stepped inside the door of the room. It was clearly stated by host and hostess that children weren't allowed. We did visit the more informal family room!

Another clear memory of this showroom-perfect home was that it was always cold in the winter. Our friends wanted to save money on their utility bills, and so the temperature during the winter was never allowed to be over 60 degrees. And you know what? There was a coldness in the family, too. The children were decent, well-behaved, beautiful, and very bright. They were praised verbally for their accomplishments throughout elementary and secondary schools. And when they graduated from high school, they could hardly wait to leave home for college. As far as I know, they never came back to live full time in that beautiful but cold house.

I remember another home. It was decorated in warmer, brighter colors, and sometimes pieces within a room might even clash! Not offensively, of course. But it wasn't perfect, wasn't photography-ready. This home, when you walked in, seemed to welcome you without words. Every chair looked comfortable and invited you to sit and relax. Of course, there were signs of life everywhere. Photographs and paintings were scattered on shelves. A book might be open on a coffee table, perhaps a few dishes waited in the sink to be placed in the dishwasher. Something was usually simmering or baking. There were occasionally toys on the carpet, and often music played on a stereo. Usually, you heard laughter or conversations from somewhere in the house, and occasionally some excited youngster ran through the door, yelling, "Hey, Mom, you gotta come see THIS!" announcing a new adventure.

Many visitors came. Sometimes unannounced, often uninvited, always welcomed with affection, perhaps dessert and a cup of coffee, many times for conversation or prayer.

Your home can be a circle of healing and warmth, of refuge,

welcome, joy and peace for your children, for your mate, and for you. It will reflect your center, your heart.

A fourth guideline, mentioned previously, is **make peace your aim.**

Let's look at some scripture verses about peace. After all, that was where our family began, and living a peaceful life became my goal.

In Chapter 1 of the book of Luke, verse 79, we are told that Jesus was sent to "guide our feet into the path of peace." In Luke 20:5-6, Jesus gives these words of instruction to his disciples as they enter a home, "When you enter a house, first say, 'Peace to this house.' If a man of peace is there, your peace will rest on him; if not, it will return to you." (NIV) Jesus also said, in John 14: 27, "Peace I leave you; my peace I give you. I do not give to you as the world gives." (NIV) I have found it true that if the Jesus-kind-of peace lives in your heart, life IS easier.

What a wonderful instruction we are given for family life in Romans 14: 19 and I want you to NOTICE this one! "Let us therefore make every effort to do what leads to peace and to mutual edification." (NIV) Peace we have heard of. It's obviously the absence of strife and destruction, whether between individuals, between nations, or within one's own mind. Perhaps "edification" is a new term. The definition of edification in the dictionary is "a building up and encouraging morally, intellectually and spiritually."

In all relationships, when you make peace and mutual encouragement your aims, you will find it greatly changes the way you deal with others.

As Jesus works to effect perfection in us, He begins to grow fruit in our personalities, and one of these fruits is peace. In Galatians 5:22, we are told, "...the fruit of the Spirit (meaning God's Holy Spirit) is love, joy, peace, patience, kindness, goodness, faithfulness, gentleness and self-control." (NIV)

In families, (as well as organizations, communities and nations!) wouldn't we get along better if we followed Jesus' advice for unity, as recorded in Ephesians 4:3, "Make every effort to keep the unity of the Spirit through the bond of peace." (NIV) **A bond of peace.** As I studied the scriptures over the years, that bond, that unifying cord, became my personal goal for my marriage, my family, and for myself.

In Colossians, Paul writes to a young church, sharing rules for holy living. The rules could certainly help our families. Let's read Colossians 3: 12-17:

> Therefore, as God's chosen people, holy and dearly loved, clothe yourselves with compassion, kindness, humility, gentleness and patience. Bear with each other and forgive whatever grievances you may have against one another. Forgive as the Lord forgave you. And over all these virtues put on love, which binds them all together in perfect unity. Let the peace of Christ rule in your hearts, since as members of one body you were called to peace. And be thankful. Let the word of Christ dwell in you richly as you teach and admonish one another with all wisdom, ...And whatever you do, whether in word or deed, do it all in the name of the Lord Jesus, giving thanks to God the Father through him. (NIV)

Peace. In your heart, your mind, and in your home. Peace can be your personal objective, your goal in your home. It was mine. It took some energy early on, thinking about ways to bring a more peaceful atmosphere to our large and active home. We placed a sign near our front gate that read, "Welcome Home" because we wanted everyone to feel welcome there, and "at home."

I wanted a home where a guest could come in, sit down, relax, and even remove his or her shoes if that seemed a comfortable thing to do "at home." I have always had the personal habit of running around in my home without my shoes. It was years later, after I'd established a "shoes off" goal that one evening it actually happened! We had invited several other couples for dinner, new friends from out of town. After the meal we adjourned to our living room for coffee and conversation in front of the fireplace. Before the evening was over I particularly noticed that one of the men, cup of coffee in hand, tipped the recliner back and quietly slipped the shoes off his feet. Not a word was said about it, until just before they were to leave.

This gentleman looked across at me and said, "I don't know when I have felt more comfortable in anyone's home. I almost hate to leave. I apologize for taking off my shoes!" I laughed and told him that he could never have known that he was paying me a great honor, and fulfilling a real desire of my heart.

Even though there were always many youngsters in our home, we decided that our family would work together to make our home a place where the tired could rest, the troubled could find healing, the angry could forgive, and the lost might be found.

One of the most important things for a family is that when Daddy or Mother (particularly, if she has employment outside the home) comes home, he or she can spend a few relaxing moments at the end of the day, reconnoitering from an encounter with the outside world. And so, for a few minutes each evening, Dad (or Mom) was allowed a short "time out" before the kids could climb all over him or hound him with their questions. We set out to make our home an oasis in a desert -- an oasis of love and acceptance.

When you think of it, our homes rather resemble green houses for plants. A planted seed sprouts into a tiny, frail plant within the safe confines of a carefully managed green house. Before we set our baby plant out in the hot summer sun, it needs to begin its growth in a place sheltered from the harshness of Mother Nature's sometimes fierce elements.

My grandmother, very early each spring, planted tomato seeds in a shallow porcelain dishpan filled with dirt sitting on her enclosed back porch. The pan of tiny plants was watered each day, and turned in the sunlight that streamed through her west windows. The plants were carefully protected until they had grown tall strong stems and could be transplanted in the garden. Even then, Grandma placed each plant carefully in the ground, sheltered from the sometimes strong Nebraska sun and wind by an empty bottomless tin can. Grandma grew the strongest, heartiest and productive tomato plants in town, probably because of the time and protective care she showered on them when they were so very tiny.

Isn't my grandmother's back porch a picture of our job as adults working with young people? We take tender young lives with the potential for as much growth and productivity as the world can offer. And we watch over each precious young person carefully, trying to protect him or her from some of the harsh winds of life, yet providing him or her some mild and limited exposure to those same forces in order for him or her to be strengthened enough to eventually face the elements without our protection. We give each of our young people precious time to grow and hopefully become strong and healthy.

Home -- a quiet, peaceful place to grow. With the goal of a peaceful home in mind, our family did not yell in the house because a loud voice was only used for an emergency. We taught our kids early on that they had "outside" voices and "inside" voices. They were not allowed to yell at each other in play, or in anger inside the house. Of course, it happened from time to time, but it was highly discouraged. As our numbers grew rapidly, it became increasingly important to follow this principle.

Not only did I expect my children to monitor their volume in our home, but I, as a mother, tried to use the tone rather than the volume of my own voice to indicate the level of seriousness when I talked to or instructed them. You may remember how it was when your own mother yelled at or called you. When her voice reached a certain volume, you knew you were in serious trouble! Of course, I never completely perfected either the inner or outer personal quietness I desired, but it was my goal, and I never gave up trying.

Today, I find that I continue similar behaviors in the classroom with high school students. Though I don't laugh as often as I used to with my family, I seldom lose my temper. And if I do, it's usually a matter of some inappropriate and disrespectful verbal comment either aimed at me or another student. And IF I feel anger, I am particularly careful NOT to raise my voice, and often times not to speak until I've regained control of any emotion I don't want to unleash. Though I may be wrong about it, showing anger or lack of self control means that I've lost the battle for living peacefully.

Another thing we did to help insure peace within our home was that we did not allow our kids to run in the house. Running, too, was an "outside" activity. And, for the most part, that was especially helpful when they were younger. We've all been in a household where tiny children run through the middle a group of grownups screaming at the top of their voices. (Usually pulling a toy, or followed by a barking puppy and screaming brother or sister, yelling, "It's MINE! Give it BACK!") Well, that just wasn't done. Our kids played -- ALL the time! -- But they did not LEGALLY run or scream in the house.

If a child (or an adult) came running through the house screaming, you knew as a parent that there was an emergency. Probably a child had some sort of "ouchie," or was reporting somebody else's mini-emergency. And with nine children from infancy to high school ages, there were OFTEN problems to report!

Now, if you're going to establish a law for the kiddos, you as an adult need to be ready to live by the rules, so a big rule for us as parents was "NO YELLING IN THE HOUSE!" (Suddenly, I am seeing the possibility of a great cartoon -- a woman yelling those words hysterically in a room full of kids! How I wish I could draw!)

The aim of keeping moderately peaceful surroundings in a home should also include a "rule" for the adults in a household, and it is this: "No fighting in front of the kids." Of course, mothers and dads will disagree about one thing or another in the course of normal living, but if we teach our children to treat each other with respect, then we need to exhibit the same policy in dealing with each other, and most certainly with them.

Each person deserves respect, even in the middle of disagreements. If you treat your friend, child, or mate with respect, the children around you learn to do the same. Or we hope they will. By the way, not yelling at your mate also means not yelling ABOUT him or her in front of the children. I did not want my kids to take sides against one parent or the other. Both parents, no matter the issue, deserve a child's respect. Parents can settle their disagreements without choosing teams!

Now, just as I have given you a principle that I believe is important, I must tell you that living this way doesn't always work perfectly. You are undoubtedly surprised, right?! Even without the yelling and screaming, kids somehow know when something is not quite right between mother and daddy. They just know.

Unfortunately, as I look back at my life, I realize that even as an only child raised in a quiet home, I felt much of the tension and unspoken conflict between my parents. What I did not understand, I imagined. And sometimes those imaginings were worse than reality.

I know that in my own home, even though my husband and I were basically polite with one another, our kids sensed unresolved tensions between us. As I look at it years later, I wonder if in our attempts to live quietly and peacefully together, to "get along," my husband and I adopted a lifestyle of non-communication, at least about the "tuff stuff," which would eventually destroy our marriage. Resolving disagreements can be accomplished with time, patience, courtesy, tenacity and quite a bit of courage.

Psychologists have understood for some time that children of chemically dependent parents often grow up with addictive or co-addictive personalities. Children who have been abandoned, or who have <u>felt</u> <u>abandoned</u>, may as adults have a difficult time establishing loving relationships within their own family. Children who have been subjected to violence or abuse will often be violent or abusive parents. Our families can have both negative AND positive influences on our own lives as parents. And that can be encouraging.

Another encouragement to me is realizing that, ultimately, my kids belong to God, and when I mess up as a parent, no matter how well intentioned I may have been, God faithfully continues to stand beside my children, helping them recover from my mistakes.

Look at the people around you. Actually, it's amazing that there are so many relatively neat and normal folks walking around, when we think of all the big and small childhood injuries they have survived.

So, as a parent, you set your priorities or goals for your family, and you do the best you can, and when you can't do any better, and you know you haven't been a perfect parent, you just have to trust God to fill in the rest.

Every parent realizes that young eyes are watching, and so we want to show our best behavior to our kids. But, in the safety of our own home, so many of our image defenses, our protective shields, our "happy faces," are down, and we end up acting out the very essence of who we ARE in front of our children.

In moments of honesty, all good intentions aside, when we least expect to, we show our children by our spontaneous actions and words, our own attitudes which undoubtedly they will consciously or subconsciously either react against or copy.

I always hate it when my kids copy the worst things about me.

Therefore, if we want to have a peaceful home, a good, quiet, and restful place for our young saplings to put down roots, receive nourishment, and grow, then we need to BE peaceful. Don't just ACT quiet. BE peaceful. Do whatever is necessary as an individual and as a couple to find a peace within yourself and between you, that will make the peace on the outside a natural action instead of a practiced, conscious one.

Does it seem to you that we are almost back to "square one?" Well, if square one is PEACE, you're probably right. For me, everything sort of centers around the inner peace that I received from the faith in Christ that I've talked about.

It's sort of like a wheel. You can't get much of anywhere without a hub, or a center. And in so much that we do, whether or not we have a strong, dependable center holding us together limits how far we travel, and how well. You may not be centered in the same things that your folks are, or I am, or anyone else you know is, for that matter. But if you have a peaceful inner self or center, it will show in your outer self.

If you planted a young sapling tree in the front yard of our little house on the Nebraska plains, where the winds blow nearly constantly from the South, you eventually had to tie it against the wind, because otherwise, left alone, the young tree would grow crooked, leaning with the wind toward the North.

In life, our young children, like young trees, lean with the wind, and if we don't help them grow strong and tall, by either taming the winds that blow around them, or restricting their "freedom" to lean with the winds, they too, may grow crooked.

Maintaining a commitment to the family, respecting each person within the family unit, and setting a goal of establishing a peaceful environment are three ways to tame the winds that blow around them.

But sometimes kids, like young trees, need to be held in place, trained and disciplined in order to grow straight and tall. Guess what we're going to talk about next!

CHAPTER 6

"Big D..Little..i..s..c..i..p..l..i..n..e!"

Discipline.

What a divisive word. It divides mother and dad, men and boys, mothers and daughters, and sergeants and privates. People have a hard time agreeing on not only what "discipline" means but also its importance in family life. We disagree on proper expectations for children, as well as the correct methods for channeling that behavior.

I remember as a younger person, hating the word discipline, and vowing I'd never use it! It was probably at a time when my mom had told me, "When you have children of your own, you'll understand why I'm doing what I am." And I determined that I would NEVER discipline like she did, and my kids would never feel what I felt, which must have been anger. Since I had very few spankings as a child, I KNOW that it wasn't physical pain from being mishandled physically.

Time passed. The wounds inflicted on my psyche by my parents trying to bend my iron will healed quickly. Before too long, I had children of my own, and rather soon I discovered that, as usual, my mother was right! Even toddlers needed to be guided and directed at an early age.

In my determination to do everything as perfectly as possible, I read Doctor Spock, Hiam Ginott, and listened to older people and other "experts" in the field of raising children. Eventually, of course, I learned that my Bible had some of the best advice about parenting. Amazingly, much of that advice has to do with my old friend, discipline.

Proverbs 22:6 -- "Train up a child in the way he should go. Even when he is old, he will not depart from it." (KJV) This reminds me of the Nebraska tree story.

Proverbs 22:15 -- "Foolishness is bound up in the heart of a child; the rod of discipline will remove it far from him." (NIV) Wait a minute! This is beginning to sound like.....

Proverbs 23:13-14 -- "Do not hold back discipline from the child. Although you beat him with the rod, he will not die. You shall beat him with the rod, and deliver his soul from hell." (NIV)

No! Not THAT!! Spanking?!

So you say to yourself, "Well, the writers of the Old Testament were small village military men. That was then. But today, we're an 'enlightened society.' We know how to raise children in our technologically advanced world with more sensitivity and understanding of their needs. Understanding is in. Spanking is out." I was certain that I was too educated, too intelligent, and too MODERN to believe in spanking children. It just isn't justified or necessary. So... that's IT!

Right? Wrong. Sometimes I think people in our "enlightened world" use such excuses to not have to do anything with their children. You know -- "Let the teachers teach them!" Many parents blame teachers when their students fail to behave properly, to talk properly, to understand the world, learn all the essentials for success, and resist the bad choices in the world.

What is discipline? It is, in the words of Proverbs, "training up." Training up is like instruction.

Talk to a horse trainer, a horticulturist, and most teachers. Young people, like any untrained young creature or young plant, must be SHOWN how to grow or behave. And that takes love, patience and lots of time. Remember the sapling growing in the Nebraska wind? Sometimes kids need more "encouragement" to grow straight and tall than a sapling on a windy prairie.

Permissive parents, unfortunately, don't want to harm their children emotionally, and so let them, early on, learn to be little tyrants. If you want to see how far children have evolved in the last two or three thousand years, put several two, three or four-year-old children in one room with a few colorful toys and no direct adult supervision, and see how well they get along.

Cooperation and kindness are NOT natural, folks! Sharing is NOT natural. Peacefulness is NOT the natural way of life. Usually, our first word is "Mine." Next comes "No" and often the loudest and biggest kid is the boss.

Raising good kids in a society that prides itself on its scientific understanding and technological advances does not take more intelligence then our ancestors had, but in the face of conflicting modern popular theories, raising good kids probably takes a considerable amount of COURAGE. If you happen to discipline your child in public, you may come under heavy criticism by observers.

Old Testament society not only encouraged a parent to discipline his children. It DEMANDED that a man discipline his children. In fact, Old Testament society said that the price for rebellion in children was <u>death</u>. Check it out. If your son rebelled, it was your duty as a loving parent to take him to the outskirts of the village and stone him! Stoning meant to throw stones at a person until he possibly died from the injuries.

Can you imagine the anguish a parent might suffer if he were forced by his society, no matter what his own child may have done to prove his rebellious nature, to kill his own flesh and blood -- publicly? In small Hebrew villages, every person knew and needed his neighbors. Every citizen had to be trustworthy. Most people were known intimately since childhood. No one admired a selfish or untrustworthy adult. And the society believed that the way you encouraged a young person to mature into a cooperative, unselfish, trustworthy adult, was to train him or her in that direction as a child. If the child refused to conform, he obviously would not conform as an adult. He was self-centered, greedy, and could not be trusted to protect the village. So they killed him, or gave him scars sufficient to remind him for the rest of his life what he needed to be in order to fit in their community.

What does this say to us? For one thing, God takes the matter of discipline and character very seriously.

Should we take it less seriously?

Jesus spent several years training adults who He hoped would eventually follow in His footsteps. And He taught them by spending time with them, by talking to them and by demonstrating in His own life the principles He wanted them to follow. They learned by walking with Him daily.

He wanted His friends to be his disciples, his "disciplined ones."

How about today? We parents are given the opportunity and responsibility of training children in a rather permissive, industrialized, technological and sophisticated society.

Oh, I don't think we should keep a pile of stones out in the yard to handle emergencies. But I do think that today's parents have often somehow been more interested in the image of "playing" parents than the responsibility of training children. We have emphasized providing things for them, and neglected time for one-on-one play and conversation with our children.

When mothers and dads look forward to the arrival of a new child, they plan and dream with pictures of trips to the beach, of rocking chairs and baby beds, of hugs, cuddling, kisses and cute clothes and family pictures for everyone to see what love can produce. We parents picture the ideal family, and somehow put ourselves in that picture. Our kids will grow up to be wonderful young people. Boys, future professional men, will grow tall and play basketball in the driveway with their dads. Girls, looking like fashion models, will learn to run a home or a business from their mothers. Parents hope their children will be intelligent, fun, good looking, popular and admired by the entire town. We believe we will always be as proud of our offspring as we are when they are tiny babies.

Sometimes, once again, reality can be quite a shock.

The cute baby realizes very early in his life that everyone in the house is interested in his or her digestion and sleep habits. The baby soon discovers that his strong demanding cry brings desired results. And before too long, he learns a most important word, "MINE!" Mother and Daddy spend the next 15 or so years trying to increase his basal vocabulary and re-center his emotional focus.

Sometimes I think the primary challenge of my life was to teach my twins boys, as well as other siblings, to share their toys without feelings of deprivation, to trust that each person would have a turn of his own with the treasure-of-the-moment, that when we fight over little things, no one really wins, and the fight becomes more important than the prize we began to fight over!

Some years ago I visited a young couple who had two tiny boys, and when the older one began bringing his favorite toys out of his room, one by one, to show me, his smaller brother followed a moment later with an identical toy. I asked the parents if they had two of every toy. And they said, "Nearly."

Since that day, I've wondered if furnishing two identical toys, or seven, if you have seven children, is a realistic way to prepare kids for life. I mean, actually, in life, we sometimes need to learn to SHARE and TAKE TURNS. Don't we?

One of the modern moves in public education in recent years is what the professionals call "Cooperative Learning," or group projects. When you look at it clearly, concisely, and away from educational jargon that reshapes old concepts into "new," what is cooperative learning other than sharing information and taking turns!?

Apparently the current move in corporate America is working within cell groups. Obviously, once again, the antique concepts of sharing strengths, ideas, and cooperation permeate our modern life.

Oh well, you have to work that out for your family. I know that my husband and I just plain didn't have the money to buy all the toys our kids wanted, and duplication simply wasn't possible. We were rather of the "old school" that said give the kids the MATERIALS for toys, and let the kids make their own. They often didn't have the fancy toys that belonged to some of their friends, but they created wonderful substitutes -- fresh and unique. Today, I can discover no real psychological distress in most of them as a result of having to learn to share and to create.

Of course, on the other hand, I do think that sometimes doing without the things you really want in childhood CAN result in adults who want EVERYTHING they see. The habit of acquiring THINGS that we think will make us happy, interestingly, if not modified as a child, may lead to a lifetime of selfish acquisition in search of an elusive happiness.

Back to discipline. Big D.

As in everything else, in order to accomplish a task, we have to determine our goals in parenting. If you are a couple, it's important, also, that you agree on these points. Remember, it takes two to live and work together harmoniously. The big question is, what sort of adults do you as a parent want to claim credit for having raised? And once you have decided the sorts of adults you admire, and wish to sire (!), then you need to decide what sorts of methods you can use for channeling or directing them in the general direction that you hope they will walk.

You and I both realize that you can more easily direct and guide your children's behaviors while they are young. Some small children respond easily to parents' instruction, rules, and guidance. Some don't, and require "time out," "withdrawal" and even stronger techniques. Eventually, each child becomes an adult who is himself responsible for his or her own choices of direction and lifestyle. And the moment of assuming individual responsibility comes at different times for different kids.

The question remains: What sort of an <u>adult</u> do you hope to produce?

For myself, I like to go back to my favorite resource, the Bible. Solomon, King David's son, the author of Proverbs which is filled with wisdom that is not only spiritual but practical, as well, had much to say about children and families.

In the dedication of Proverbs, Chapter One, Solomon explains why the Word of God and particularly the Proverbs of Solomon (a wise father) are important:

They teach wisdom and self-control.
They give understanding.

They will teach you how to be wise and self-controlled.
They will teach you what is honest and fair and right.
They give the ability to think to those with little knowledge.
They give knowledge and good sense to the young.
Wise people should also listen to them and learn even more.
Even smart people will find wise advice in these words.
Then they will be able to understand wise words and stories.
They will understand the words of wise men and their riddles.
Knowledge begins with respect for the Lord,
But foolish people hate wisdom and self control.
My child, listen to your father's teaching.
And do not forget your mother's advice.
Their teaching will beautify your life.
It will be like flowers in your hair or a chain around your neck.
(Proverbs 1:2-9 -- *International Children's Bible*, NCV)

Our desire (Well, MY desire!) was to train up children who became wise, though not necessarily in the so-called sophisticated wisdom presented by the world, and so often available via mass media. Rather than the self-centered pursuit of temporary satisfaction or acquiring things, our desire was to raise a mature, good, sensitive and sensible adult who becomes a man or woman others appreciate for his or her wisdom in both action and counsel.

Kids do not just BECOME good and wise by OSMOSIS, by absorbing the goodness and wisdom of those around them, or the books we give them to read. Kids need to be taught and guided into maturity. A small child is a self-centered little tyrant, even though he may be a beautiful, cuddly tyrant who "looks just like his daddy!" A child does not by nature share, or think of another person's happiness.

For a baby, or a small child, or a big child who has never grown up, (and I'm certain you've met a few of THEM!) the center of the universe is ME. Part of maturity is realizing that the world does not revolve around ME. Sometimes it hurts to realize that.

According to *Webster's Unabridged Dictionary*, possessing wisdom means being wise. And a person who is wise "distinguishes and judges soundly concerning what is true or false, proper or improper; choosing the best ends and the best means for accomplishing them." Being wise is the complete opposite of being foolish.

A foolish person, on the other hand, is "silly or unwise in his or her dealings." A fool shows lack of good judgment both in choosing his goals and his steps to get there -- both the ends and means for accomplishing them.

Growing up means learning that I am not the center of the world I live in, but part of a whole. Either I, as a part of the whole, help or hurt the whole by my attitude. And I am responsible for my actions and reactions.

Perhaps, when I was little, if my mother had caught me hitting my brother's head with a plastic Tinker Toy stick (if I'd had a brother!), I might have said, "It's his fault! He hit me first!" Or, "He took my tricycle!" I am grown now. I can't always blame my bad attitude or my bad actions on other people or events. I am responsible for myself. No matter what happens around me. My actions and my words, my choices are mine.

Interestingly, children do not stop thinking or talking or behaving like little children unless we help them along. If parents don't insist, children will not brush their teeth. They will not pick up their own toys. They will not share, because they don't WANT to share. They will usually not eat the vegetables that are good for them (neither will some adults I know!)

Children, untaught, undisciplined, (particularly in a culture that is afraid of gray hair, tummy bulges and wrinkles) will not naturally respect their elders. And, if parents can be manipulated by their children, children will not respect their parents.

Like it or not, when a child begins, he is not wise. Therefore, he is foolish. He is unable to distinguish bad from good, unable to choose the best goals, and the best ways to reach those goals. Proverbs 22:15 says, "Foolishness is bound up in the heart of a child; the rod of discipline will remove it far from him." (KJV)

The Bible speaks of disciplining or training, with a tool called a rod. What is a rod? A rod is an instrument used by shepherds (check the 23rd Psalm -- "Thy rod and thy staff, they comfort me." -- KJV) and other early tribal people to correct, to defend, and to fight if need be. Simply put, it was a stick.

Isn't it interesting that Jesus called Himself "The Good Shepherd?" In so many ways, He is, and if we have followed His teaching, we parents try to become "good shepherds" as we "train up" our own children.

Shepherds, when guiding sheep, reached out with their rod and tapped their dumb but skittish sheep on the outside shoulder to keep them from wandering off the path. A good shepherd didn't yell at his sheep, because he knew that sheep were frightened very easily by noises. Instead, he "spoke softly and carried a big stick." The reminder by an attentive shepherd helped the flock learn to avoid danger, and the tap on the shoulder of an easily-frightened sheep usually caused a quick response. Any hesitation or delay in the sheep's moving to the safest position as they walked along meant the sheep was in danger.

Sheep were comforted by the tap of the shepherd's long stick, which, when heeded, kept the short-sighted sheep in the safety of the fold and away from unnoticed danger. It reminded them to stay close to the shepherd, who was strong enough to battle lions and wolves for the sake of his defenseless flock and who watched over them protectively.

In our rather permissive society, is it possible for our children, like little lambs, to be "comforted' by the tap of their parent's "rod?" I believe, if applied correctly, the "rod of correction" is a sign of love that will comfort and assure our children of our loving concern for them.

Again, let's go back to Proverbs 13:24, and we hear King Solomon say, as recorded in *The Message Bible*, "A refusal to correct is a refusal to love; love your children by disciplining them."

I have no idea the number of times I said to my children, as I prepared to demonstrate my love in correction, "I love you too much to let you act in this unacceptable manner." Loving parents keep their children out of the streets so that they will not be destroyed by the traffic racing by. When we have rules and guidelines for our children, it's like building fences around the yard where they play, to protect them. If a young child climbs over the fence, the watchful adult hurries to bring him back into the safety of his yard. And we talk (loudly, perhaps) to him (or her), trying to make him know he's not to continue the potentially harmful behavior.

Of course, at the time of the correction, the rod does not FEEL really comforting. I mean, a spanking hurts! But sometimes we need it. Perhaps you may remember a television commercial for an aftershave a few years ago, where the model slapped himself on the cheeks with the lotion, shook his head, and said, "Thanks. I needed that!" Even after a slap that we need, though we may be a bit stunned or even upset, our response, when we know it was deserved or necessary, will eventually be the same.

When the majority of our children were young, and we were first learning some of the principles of Christian discipline, we posted a big bulletin board in our dining room. And from time to time, among the pictures and souvenirs, we put new scriptures we were learning. In the middle of this bulletin board were our basic house rules for using the rod of correction. We took the time to explain to our kids the grounds for a spanking. They were:

Rebellion

Disrespect

Disobedience

Any of these three, whether in look, word or deed, would call for the application of discipline. Our intention was to accept the responsibility for training our children to be good, wise, obedient and respectful young people. And they were being taught, hopefully, to walk in the way they should grow.

If a child was told to perform a task that he (or she) was entirely capable of performing, but he refused to perform, he was spanked. If the child did the task, but did it in anger, or especially slowly or reluctantly, and was very obvious about the anger and rebellion, he or she was spanked. The child had to learn to obey quickly, his father's (or mother's) voice. If he acted in a disrespectful manner to another person, no matter what the cause, out came the old rod again! I can hear what you may be thinking. "With nine or ten kids, they must have been spanking every two minutes! What barbarians!"

True, for a short while, when we first started trying to "get it together," it seemed that we were spanking kids more often than we had earlier. But before very long, they learned to act in an appropriate manner the majority of the time. And, before very long, too, it seems we just didn't spank often at all.

Actually, in the last few years of raising children, my older kids tell me that we didn't spank the littler ones as often as we should have! They thought we had become lax once again. And they may have been right. We just seem to have gotten out of the habit of using that form of discipline, and many times older siblings verbally corrected and taught the younger children before Mom or Dad had a chance to do it.

One of the stories my older kids recently reminded me about was of the day long ago, when they had all gotten in trouble for something that no one remembers doing. They were told to line up in the living room for Dad to spank each of them in turn, starting with the oldest. At the time, we did not have an official "rod" -- later we did. So, Dad started with the oldest, Randy, gave a swat or two on his behind as Randy "grabbed his ankles," and promptly broke the ping pong paddle right in two!

Everyone laughed!

But Dad, always resourceful, told everyone to stay put and went downstairs to the basement family room to get another one! Kevin was the youngest in line at the time and stood at the end of the line of kids. When Dad returned to the lineup, fresh ping pong paddle ready for action, while the others stifled their giggles, and accepted their punishment one-by-one, Kevin started bawling at the top of his lungs, trying to get his Dad to take pity on him.

"Did it work?" I asked.

Everyone laughed uproariously, and said, "No!"

Obviously, the memory of our discipline sessions did not injure them very seriously.

As young parents, we established some guidelines for ourselves in spanking our kids. And I generally feel they are good ones that others might appreciate, too.

The first rule for parents was that we NEVER spanked a child while we were still angry with him or her. It is too dangerous for a big person to express anger or frustration at a smaller person. If the child's misbehavior caused us anger, then we talked to them, and made a promise to spank later when were calmer.

You see, the purpose of applying the "rod of correction," is to enforce the policies of the family, for the good of the individual, not to injure either their body or their ego.

The second rule for parents was that we always used an instrument for the physical correction -- a "rod." It seems, scripturally, that parental discipline was enforced by a stick. Never use the bare hand. Hands, we felt, were meant to express love. Parents' hands brush hair, button buttons, cuddle kids, pat them when they need to be comforted, and carry them inside the house when they fall asleep in the car. Hands love.

I never wanted my child to flinch when I reached out to touch him. Over years as I looked around, I have noticed with sorrow children who respond to a quick move of an adult's hand with fear. Usually, there is some reason for such fear.

Peterson's third rule for parents was to follow established guidelines for both parents and children.

Naturally, the children had to know the rules. A child was not to be corrected for things he or she had never understood. Our rules and daily chores were posted on the bulletin board. When a kid broke the house rules, he (or she) was aware of it beforehand, usually, and if that was true, we determined that he should be responsible for his actions. When it came time for a spanking, we usually followed a format similar to this:

1. Explain the rule that was broken, getting the child to agree that there was a rule, and he or she had neglected to follow it.
   Example:

   Mom -- "Do we hit our brothers and sisters?"
   Junior -- (eyes downcast) "No...But he...took my truck."
   Mom -- "Okay, we'll take care of his mistake later. Now,

what about you? Who controlled your hand? Your brother,
or you?"
Junior -- (probably reluctantly) "Me.
Mom -- "And so, who should be disciplined for hitting?"
Junior -- "Me."
Mom -- "Right. Okay, grab your ankles.

I must take a moment here to say that it does seem somehow
inconsistent to me for adults to punish violence using violence.
And, so, my spankings were, at least from my perspective, not a
moment of violence. I spent considerably more time talking to the
"perpetrators," and reassuring them that I loved and believed in
them than I did spanking them.

2. Give appropriate number of swats. What is the appropriate
   number? Our idea was that we spanked until the kid was
   willing to admit that it hurt, submitted his or her resistance,
   and usually cried. Many times, the older kids don't want you
   to know that you are hurting them, even if the swats are only
   hurting their pride, and it takes a little more "encouragement"
   or muscle for them to become tearful. I didn't check for tears
   on the cheeks, but for tears in the eyes -- not of anger, but
   that an impression had been made that we "meant business"
   with the rules, as well as the swats.

Is this a clear description of our goals and our strategies?
Perhaps it may sound a little crazy to you to wait for submission,
or tears.
I am reminded of a white-haired nurse in a small hospital who
was caring for me during the last stages of my labor with Kevin.
I had been walking the floor for an hour or so, and knew that the

time was near for the baby's arrival. I asked the nurse who had been attending births for over 40 years to call the doctor.

She took a close look at my face (which wasn't the part of me hurting, for crying out loud!), and said, "Old Dr. Warren always said to wait until I saw the tears before I called him." I, who had steeled myself for years, NOT to cry when in pain, had to submit to the pain I felt, and had to let her SEE the pain in my eyes before she called the doctor.

Was she right? Who knows!? All I know is that by the time the doctor, who had been mowing his lawn a few blocks away, arrived at the hospital, he barely had the time to wash his hands and catch Kevin, who the doctor thought was big enough to be a "baby elephant!" If I'd have submitted to the labor pains a little sooner, maybe they'd not have lasted so long!

If you take the time to know your child well, and not just his or her behavior patterns, you are probably able to look the child in the eyes and know a little about what is going on in his or her mind. The eyes, after all, are "the window to the soul." Take the time to look; it's important to respond to what you see. And, I believe it is important that we let our kids look into our eyes, too. I suspect that occasionally when my children were looking at me during a discipline session, they saw tears in my eyes, too.

3. Another principle of disciplining with a "rod" that we tried to follow was to apply the rod ONLY to the "seat of knowledge." Spank only on the portion of the anatomy that is padded for the purpose! If a child wears padded clothing (like thick undies, or big thick pull-up toddler diapers, etc.) and is old enough to know the error of his way, lower the drawers to expose the cheeks for a couple of swats. The purpose is not to impress the child with the noise of swatting

thick clothing, but rather to make an impression on his mind by reminding his flesh about the consequences of forgetting the rules.

I never wanted to hit or slap a child in the face, on the head, or anywhere else on the body, intentionally, either with a hand or another instrument. That is anger. And it is abuse. Of course, I must confess that there have been a few times when a swat hit a child on the legs because the child rebelled against receiving the correction, and wiggled away.

The purpose of spanking is not to injure or bruise, but rather that the child learns to submit his will to his parents, and eventually to others in authority in his life. That's why our kids learned to bend over and grab their ankles or bend over a table or couch to be spanked. The action is a sign of them taking responsibility for their behavior and submitting to the correction.

There is a move in modern families away from old-fashioned respect for ANY kind of authority figure. Some children have heard more about their "rights" than their "responsibilities" very early in life, and many of them have very obviously had no form of correction. I'm afraid this will possibly have a devastating effect on generations in the future -- generations of young self-centered teens and adults who refuse to take the responsibility for their own success or failure and continue to say as they grow up, what one petulant teen told me just recently: "My mother told me I could have anything I wanted because I'm special!"

On the other hand, there also seems to be a swing back to older more stable "family" values in our country among the more conservative element. I hope so, because a generation of future parents with the selfish attitude of this little girl could be very destructive for the next round of children.

4. The fourth part of our discipline process was that after the correction was applied, and duly noted by the recipient, it was time for reconciliation. You know, the old "now that I have your attention, let's talk" routine!

There are two major things that need to be shared in the communication sessions following applying the appropriate corporal punishment -- love and forgiveness.

Initially, after correction had been given, it was very important that our children realized that we loved them, and that we had spanked them because we took our job seriously. Not that we enjoyed making their fannies hurt!

Somehow, kids had to accept their responsibility to conform to family policy, and they had to accept the fact that parents are commanded by God to train or teach them, and, sometimes to discipline them.

In the second part of our reconciliation, it was very important that parent and child, following our private "session," forgive one another. I asked my child to forgive me for spanking him, though I did not apologize for it. I just didn't want my child to believe that I enjoyed it, and I knew that our relationship could continue if he or she forgave me. Also, I forgave him, and said so, for his poor choice or behavior. I told my child that I loved him (or her). And I asked for a hug. Sometimes it took a short period of time before the child could fairly freely express love for me. But we tried, and usually, we got there pretty quickly.

The goal of parenting and training children is to raise children who, early on, accept the responsibility for their behavior, and begin early to make good decisions. Remember that when we train up a child in the way he should go, we are promised that he will not stop making wise decisions.

Unfortunately, many modern parents believe that their own permissiveness is an expression of love, though it really isn't love at all. And what they struggle to understand, spanking, in many respects, when used correctly, is an excellent expression of love. I used to call it TOUGH LOVE.

I remember my dear old friend Lynn, a minister who had never married, and though much loved by others' children, never raised children of his own, laughing and saying to me as he watched me "in action," "Oh, Linda, you are TOO honest! Sometimes you just should NOT tell the truth!"

Lynn, in order to get along with people, thought it better to ignore inappropriate behavior in children and adults than to address it. He never wanted to talk to anyone about the way he truly felt, or about what he expected from others. He had decided years before to avoid permanent ties (like marriage) because, somehow, he was afraid he'd be disappointed or hurt. We all loved him dearly, but I felt sad that he missed so much of the best life offers us because he was afraid to take many chances in his personal life.

I am not afraid. I am not afraid of loving, and I am not afraid of letting you see who I really am. I am not afraid that I will lose you if I tell you truth. And if I do lose a relationship with you, then I never really HAD one. I am not afraid of telling you that you are standing on my toe. I am not afraid of saying to the children who have been given to my care, that I love them too much to allow them to have a twisted sense of the center of the universe.

I did not let my little children tear up my house. I did not let my big children tear up my life. I tried to teach them to submit their will, for the most part, to the needs of the greater cause – the family. And, as I've stated before, the greater need within our household was to keep REAL peace and harmony. And I was not afraid to apply necessary discipline measures when peace and harmony within my home had been destroyed by the selfish desires and actions of a little or a bigger tyrant.

Now, in all this tough talk, I realize that I probably sound a little like "Machine Gun Annie." But I think that my children consider me rather the opposite. They may or may not remember my swats. But I KNOW that they remember their DAD'S spankings! He talked less but spanked harder! Our kids will probably remember SOME of my words. And I believe they still know that both of us, however imperfectly, loved them very much.

Since I have discussed the matter of discipline at some length, and have given you some of the guidelines we used in raising our kids, I think it is time to present some important thoughts about the "middle way" -- moderation.

We took our job as parents seriously. We expected our kids to listen as we instructed them, and because they trusted our love for them, to obey our instructions to them. We expected good behavior from our kids, not because they were angels in disguise, but because they were good kids. We knew that they were still just people, and people make mistakes, sometimes intentionally, sometimes not.

But in the matter of physical discipline, I think, we took a "middle way" with them. We did spank. And when we first began developing the "system" I outlined previously, we were probably tougher then in later years, and that appears to be true. We did expect obedience, but we did not use our responsibilities as parents as an excuse to dominate weaker people and have our own way. We did NOT attempt in any way to break their wonderful spirits. We were not overly harsh with them in expecting appropriate behavior, but rather expressed, time and again, our appreciation of each child's uniqueness.

Also, and it should be understood without saying, when we expected our children to perform in an appropriate manner, WE also behaved appropriately. If we asked them to be quiet and peaceful and respectful in our home, then we parents needed to remain quiet and peaceful and respectful in the home. EVEN when we were disciplining them.

Using the same "behavior yard stick" means that if they may not yell at one another, we also did not yell at one another. As a matter of fact, we, for the most part, considered yelling a sign in an adult of the loss of self control, and the preamble to violence that we deplored. When we disciplined our children, we did not yell at them -- or if we were mad enough to yell at them, we certainly knew that we were too angry to spank.

Also, when we corrected the inappropriate behavior or attitudes of our kids, we had to be certain not to demean them, or "put them down." The purpose of discipline is to effect behavior and attitude, not to break the precious spirit of a child. We did not want him to think that he was a worthless piece of junk that we parents just had to put up with. We did not want to cause him or her excessive anger, either at us, or at himself. It is a well-known fact that kids who have been disciplined either too harshly or perhaps without love, or not disciplined at all, grow up with some rather strange attitudes about life, especially when it comes time to parent their own children.

The Bible, in the *New International Version*, says in Ephesians 6:4 "...fathers, do not provoke your children to anger; (The King James Version calls that anger "wrath.") but bring them up in the discipline and instruction of the Lord."

Colossians 3:21 says it differently, "Fathers, do not embitter your children, or they will become discouraged." (NIV)

Just as the middle way is important when it comes to preventing OVER disciplining kids, the middle way is also important when it comes to the other extreme -- permissive parenting.

I am reminded of a small family we once knew very well and

loved as dear friends. Mother and father were wonderful, gentle, kind, intelligent and sincere Christian people. However, for various reasons, they were extremely permissive with their one daughter. The father was particularly so. When the little girl, long after she was able, failed to pick up her crayons when told to, daughter whined, and father picked them up, usually finding some excuse for his daughter's inability (which was actually her unwillingness) to conform to any request.

As time passed, parents often fixed two meals -- one for them, and one for their daughter. Over the years, they continually excused her increasingly deplorable behavior and her lack of friends her own age, with amazing, unbelievable blindness to the nasty, spoiled, self-serving young person she was becoming.

Interestingly, the daughter, moving into adolescence, became more and more dependent upon her parents, and less and less respectful. Her disrespect was quiet, but it was very obvious to a neutral observer that she, so very well taught scriptural principles, did not honor her parents. After all, she was a very bright girl, quite pretty, who had been able to manipulate both of her parents, and particularly her father, ever since she was very tiny. Whenever her mother tried to correct her, she called out, "Daaaaad!" And Dad intervened, rescuing her from her mother's slightest firmness.

One day mother and father tried to get their daughter, then about 10, to leave our house before she was ready to go home. They stood on either side of her, and literally lifted her like a big whining rag doll from the carpet. They threatened, cajoled, laughed and even raised their voices before finally giving her a couple of "baby swats" through her winter coat and other heavy layers of clothing, while she whined and resisted limply. Eventually, extremely embarrassed, they dragged her out the door, stuffed her unceremoniously in their car and left. Now, you tell me who YOU think won that round!? It was a very, very sad, moment for my shocked children to watch.

What happened to this family? Well, in spite of their rather extreme family dynamics, I guess they turned out okay. Daughter, now grown and married, may never be able to live far from her doting parents. Of course, mother and father may ALWAYS have a psychological adolescent on their hands. I have never really understood, though I love them dearly, how their crippling behavior with their child could be interpreted as love. To me, it was destructive and sad -- for all of them.

For myself, I'd rather have a little "tough love" mixed in with understanding and loving compassion. Of course there are lots of reasons why kids misbehave and fail to meet our expectations, and we parents need to be open to listening to what our kids have to tell us about themselves and their behavior.

But when it comes to the process of growing up, kids also need to be given ample opportunity to mature in the areas of taking responsibility for their actions, their thoughts, and their words. This process takes time. It takes a few spankings, a few blank walls to run up against, a few instant rewards for choices -- both good and bad -- some successes and some failures along the path of childhood, to learn to walk like a wise and responsible adult. Let's face it, when we, as parents, fail to "train up" our children, eventually, life itself will provide training experiences to help them learn the life lessons they need.

You might say that childhood and adolescence are like a junior version of "on the job training!" You learn to ride a bicycle, initially, not without using handlebars, or in the middle of a bicycle race, but alone with the personal guidance of someone who knows how to ride a bicycle. Your teacher may give you a shove, and may run alongside, holding on to the back of the bicycle seat while you learn to balance.

The process of learning to balance may take a long time and many "runs." However, because you have someone who is stronger and smarter, helping you balance, running alongside, you are not afraid of falling over. But one day, one fine day, you grow up and don't need that firm hand on your bicycle seat any longer. You stand alongside your coach, ready to take off. He says, "You can do it. I know you can!" After you climb on the seat, he gives you a little shove, letting go of the bicycle. And, if you were trained well, you, without assistance, ride your bike all by yourself!

Life is rather like that. We parents have kids for a few developing years, early in their life. Then one day, after lots of time as the coach, running alongside, we stand on the curb and watch our young people leave us and live on their own. They ride proudly away, joyfully, while we watch with tears in our hearts. And a block or so away, before they are completely out of sight, they turn around and peddle back past us, so that we can admire the results of our hard work, grinning and waving proudly.

What a thrill it is to stand on the curb, grinning and waving back at smiling young adults as they sail smoothly past, one-by-one, hollering, "Hey, look at me, Mom!! I can do it! By myself! NO HANDS!"

And the neat thing is that over the years that follow, adult kids keep riding around the block, keep checking in whenever they feel the need to either share their success, or check in for a little encouragement, guidance, or maybe just a hug from the old "coach."

CHAPTER 7

Maintaining the Middle Way, or Lighten Up!

The Ancient Greeks believed the moderate path in life was the way of perfection, and in so many ways, I absolutely agree with them.

Let's say you are a parent in today's rapidly-changing world.

You read the words of child psychologists, therapists and other "experts" about the things you need to do for your kids. Many modern-day parents try to do everything perfectly, providing all their children's real or imagined needs. Not only do they sometimes hurt themselves trying to be perfect parents and raise perfect children in an imperfect world, but often good intentions, taken to extremes, also hurt their kids.

I watch kids who have more toys than they can play with in a year, who have a television in their bedroom to entertain them, computers in order to talk to strangers all evening long behind their closed bedroom door, and after-school activities that entertain, exhaust and either disappoint them or create false hopes about their futures as dancers, athletes, artists, etc. Parents work overtime to provide all they think their children may need, and miss out knowing the kids themselves. Meals are eaten separately, and dedicated conversation or play times just evaporate away.

That is why, as we continue, I want to tell you that, as we talk about different needs in children's lives, you need to relax about the "rules." The encouraging thing I often remind myself is that children, growing into adults, are wonderfully resilient, are filled with more strength than we could have hoped, and will usually turn into amazingly secure adults, sometimes in spite of our less-than-perfect efforts as parents.

So, when I miss the mark I've aimed for, when I blow my "Super Mom" image, yell at my kids or the dog, or the washing machine, or run through the house fuming hysterically because my husband used my favorite old, "perfectly good" flannel housecoat to wax the car, well, what are we going to do? Throw in the towel? Forget the dreams we dreamed about a great, loving, peaceful family? Knowing that we have blown all our plans for perfection, shall we just give up and send the kids to reform school to let the system train them!?

NO!

NEVER GIVE UP!

So I blew it. We all blow it. It happens. And I'll probably blow it again before I get over today's mistake. But I still want to try.

I need to be honest with myself, and with my family. Honest enough to say, "Well, guys, I blew it...again." I mean, let's face it; our kids <u>know</u> when we fail to meet our own expectations. Why should we try to hide it, or defend our actions?

Instead, how much better it would be if we learn one of the most important lessons in life -- When everything seems to have fallen apart -- when all else fails -- take a deep breath -- and -- LAUGH!

The Bible says about laughter, "A merry heart doeth good like a medicine." (Proverbs 17:22 –KJV) Laughter from a merry heart is the greatest "middler of the road" that I know. Laughter at ourselves

(NOT someone else!) in the middle of a muddle is a wonderful tool to bring us down from that lofty perch of perfection upon which we parents often feel we must sit. It somehow balances things out when we are able to pull back from the serious situations we deal with as parents, and relax enough to admit that we are still learning each day how to **be** parents, as well as, for many of us, how to follow Christian principles and be a PERSON.

There are many kinds of laughter in this world. But the kind I am speaking about is the kind that reflects joy in the heart, a sense of pulling away from the little frustrating brush fires we must put out each day, the so-called everyday emergencies.

How do you find happiness and joy and cheer in the middle of chronic problems? I don't know. Sing. Read something you love. Leave the job unfinished and go lay in a hammock for awhile. Take a nap. Get your nails done. Go visit someone you haven't seen since graduation. Drive the car down a country road you haven't explored before, with the windows wide open and singing full-volume with the radio.

Whatever brings you joy, laughter, and the perspective you need, DO!! There is no problem so big that having a good sense of humor about yourself wouldn't help.

When the Bible tells us that each Christian is to "work out your own salvation" (Philippians 2:12), we might also add that each parent is daily working out, or putting into practice, his parenting priorities, and each marriage partner is working out the daily aspects of his marriage commitment.

In life, when we attach each little detail with such importance that we are not able to laugh at our failures and occasional foolishness, life will eventually become much too heavy to enjoy, no matter how many accomplishments you have, how many big person toys you earn, or awards sit in your son or daughter's trophy cabinet.

Undoubtedly, we have each known people who have become so engrossed in their pursuit of money, love, things -- you name it -- who seem to have lost all sense of perspective, all joy in living, all enjoyment of life.

First, the smile goes, then they begin to droop physically, and their voice becomes more of a whine or moan. And, unfortunately, sometimes they just quit living because their problems seem so much bigger than anyone else's, and certainly bigger than they think they can handle.

Our misfortunes shouldn't isolate us. They are just further symptoms of living in this not-so-perfect, topsy-turvy world of ours.

Things go wrong. Children. Marriages. Health. Careers. You name it. And sometimes you or I will be standing right nag dab in the middle of it all — maybe we'll have accidentally CAUSED things to go wrong.

Unfortunately, it happens.

So, dear ones, don't be afraid to laugh. Laugh at yourself and trust God. Trust that things will get better somehow, and that our kids will still turn out okay, even when we blow it.

Now, here's a thing about laughter. You may laugh at yourself. And you may laugh with another person who is also laughing at his own folly. However, whatever you do, **do NOT laugh at your children when they are not laughing at themselves.** It does some cruel things to our children's self esteem when their moms and dads laugh at them. We're dealing with some tender young egos here, and I just don't know any child that enjoys being the center of a grown up's jokes. No child wants to be "put down."

I believe the best example of self-deprecating humor was shown in the work of comedian Red Skelton, who told a joke, or did a character skit, and then laughed at himself while everyone in the audience laughed with him. What a delightful man. Who could be mad at or even put down a man who seemed to see himself so clearly and with such a light heart.

Kids feel that way, too. When mothers and fathers take themselves and their job so terribly intensely that no one can enjoy the family, it's hard on their kids. Keep things fairly light as often as you can. Laugh with a gentle and forgiving heart. And, as much as you can, believe that there are happy endings -- even for regular folks like you and me.

I will never forget the hot summer evenings after Rod got home from a long day building other people's houses when we piled all 9 and sometimes more kids in our van and headed to "cool off" at the swimming and picnic area of a nearby state park. Often we took a picnic dinner and hotdogs for the built-in barbecue grill, and spent several fun hours playing together, laughing, splashing, swimming or wading in the cool water. The sound of children's laughter, the wet-towel hugs and hollers from a bigger kid showing off — "Hey, Mom!! Look at THIS!" fill my mind with smiling thoughts and a thankful heart.

CHAPTER 8

"Seasoned with Love"

Over the years, I've noticed that there are many kinds of love. I've also noticed that love is not multiplied or divided according to traditional mathematical formulas.

At birth, we weren't each given a bushel of love pills, and when you run out, you won't ever love again. Love is available to us, and often through us, from day one until that last day.

I suspect it's true, however, that you may have a different measurement for assessing that love than the person next to you. Certainly, some individuals just find it easier than others to love.

I personally believe, however, that love, the RIGHT kind of love, is a gift from God, and comes along in a package when you ask Him Who best "loved the world" to give you more.

Some people asked us as our family grew, "How could you find room in your heart for all those children?" The answer is that it doesn't take more love to love 3 or 7 or 9 children than it does to love one. Of course, it takes more energy to take care of more kids. As a matter of fact, we discovered that love, given away somehow wonderfully, even magically, multiplies itself and grows stronger the more times it is shared with children. Love, as it becomes older, may change-- mature, become more or less forgiving, etc. But you can never give away all the love you were given in your own package. At least I don't think you can! It hasn't run out for me, as yet, and I've been lovin' lots of kids for lots of years!

Our family has been a particularly clear example of the multiplication principle. We began with two adults (or so we thought!) and multiplied to produce two children, Melissa and Kevin. An unplanned but much welcomed surprise package gave us a third child, Katie. Because of our own abundance of spirit, I guess, we began believing there was "still room for one more" and we welcomed Ricky. After several "borrowed" or foster kids came for short periods of time, Randy, Kathy and John came forever. Our longest term foster son, "Randy Mac" was with us for two years of his adolescence, and then the totally amazing gift of four-month-old twin baby boys, Andrew and David, completed our full house.

No one could have been happier than I was as a young mother. That doesn't mean that I had it "all together," in any respect. But I loved being able to stay home, and make our nest comfortable for the family, and for anyone else who came for dinner, for a day, and sometimes for a month or two. In fact, I remember once realizing that I could think of no more than 3 evening meals in the year before that particular moment that we had served to ONLY our family of 11. It seemed there were always "extras" in our home, campers parked in our driveway, or someone extra bunking briefly in the extra bedroom.

Because our hearts were open to the relationships that were created from bonds other than blood, people came to us and telephoned us any time of the day or night, from any part of the country. It was an amazing time for all of us. And I suspect it was amazing, perhaps even puzzling for those who watched us from another home or neighborhood.

Many people expressed amazement at the acceptance and welcome in our home. And we were often asked if we didn't feel that we were somehow cheating our "own" children by the life we lived.

I suspect my grown kids, looking back at what seems to me busy but wonderful days, may have different answers than mine to the question of feeling cheated. Though we were not rich, and sometimes couldn't afford to buy everything they individually may have wanted, I don't think they were particularly short-changed when it came to love.

I say this because though I felt at the time that there were more blessings than difficulties in having a "Welcome Home" sign by our front gate, I realize now that the grown children in my family may have experienced some feeling of loss somewhere along the line. Certainly, it is a possibility.

I am reminded of an American Christian missionary couple we met in India who had lived for more than 30 years among the predominately Hindu people. This couple had two grown sons who had been sent away from their parents to mission schools for the majority of their elementary and secondary education. As a teen, one of the boys had been killed in an automobile accident in India. And the other boy, grown, a college graduate living in the United States, according to his mother, still wept bitterly each time he was forced to say goodbye to his parents.

This beautiful woman looked me in the eye (at that time we hoped to also be sent as missionaries to live in India) and said, "The people who will pay for your calling from God will be your children." I wanted to argue with her. But I couldn't. She was the person who had lived what she said. Surely, I would not allow my children to feel bitter about the choices in my life which were based on what I felt God wanted me to do.

As time went along, I remembered her warning and began taking note of other families whose parents lived a life of the "fanatic," both as religious and political leaders. Though I <u>wanted</u> this lady to be overstating her point, I began to realize that there was certainly truth in what she had told me. Time and time again over the last 20-plus years, I have seen beautiful young people, teens, usually, angry at their parents and even at God because they felt somehow short-changed by their parents, or by God.

Though I do not personally feel that my children suffered substantial losses because of our large family, I can see where some of what happened in our lives might have left them with some unshed tears, or some unresolved needs. I suspect that's true of most families, of any size or composition.

Certainly, if I were parenting younger kids today, the one thing I would spend more energy with is devoting real quality time to each individual child. I TRIED to do it. I had read about Mrs. Susannah Wesley, mother of early Methodist church leaders Charles and Jonathan and 11 or 12 others, and I kept her child-rearing principles on my own bulletin board to remind me of my own priorities. One of Mrs. Wesley's rules was to spend a few minutes ALONE with each child each week. And I tried to do that, too, unofficially.

But I am sure, no matter how I tried, that I failed to fulfill all their needs for good mothering. I know that several of them at times resented having to share bedrooms and toys, as well as Mother and Dad's time. However, when they get together now, it is not to complain, but to laugh at the funny memories they have of times shared together. For we made a concerted effort to play together and work together. I limited television time, and forced them to spend time together. Generally, it was quite successful, or seemed so. And, when it balances out, I hope they will feel it was all worth it.

When I see one of my children or grandchildren in need, and we have had many moments when they needed each other, I'm blessed beyond words to know that two, three or four brothers or sisters will be alongside, helping out their siblings. I've seen them come together to support one another in some very difficult times. I've watched them embracing one another, carrying physical and emotional burdens to help one another. I've seen them cry with helplessness, knowing their brother or sister, niece or nephew, might be in pain, and there are no easy answers.

It's called love. And when given freely, it flows in abundance. In fact, it multiplies.

I know it. I've seen it. I've lived it.

CHAPTER 9

"Special Kids"

In life, sometimes we use the word "special" to mean handicapped. And, no matter how you look at it, in our family, our mentally handicapped son, Ricky, was "special." Many times, I described our family as the "family that Ricky built." His beautiful spirit, his pure love for every person he ever met, his joy in living a simple life with his bicycle, good food and lots of hugs, and his instant forgiveness of any person who may have needed it -- all these things taught us.

Ricky had no words to preach. He only lived to love. Our life together began with a newspaper picture of a little boy sitting sideways in a wooden wagon, and an article about this little foster boy in our town who, because his foster parents were about to retire, welfare workers sought to place in a new foster home. At the time, we were proud and busy parents of three small children. Melissa (then called "Missy") was five, Kevin was four, Katie had just turned two in April, and Ricky would be six in early November.

A friend in our church, Judy, saw the picture, and handed it to me one September morning, and said, "When I saw this, I thought of you." (I had obviously told her about Jo and *Little Women*!)

I still have that article, with his caseworker's telephone number written hastily in the margin. Within six weeks, Ricky was part of our young family. Just in time to celebrate his birthday.

And he WAS special. I cannot briefly tell you the amazing number of growing experiences that came to me because of him. He accepted life as it was, moment by moment, usually joyfully. He was best at enjoying each day fully, and he helped us learn to do the same. Though I saw him afraid, sad and hurt on occasion, I never saw Ricky become sarcastic or bitter or vindictive. And that is a remarkable legacy.

Profoundly retarded and "non-verbal" seem like big words when one decides to be a foster and then an adoptive parent for a child. But, somehow, it seemed to me then, and even more so today, that Ricky was wiser than all of us. And he was a wonderful communicator. Early on, we prayed that he'd be "healed" and receive language, thinking it would be a spoken language. As time passed, he did learn to say a few elementary words, but eventually, we realized that spoken language was not his choice. Something spontaneous might slip out of his mouth that we understood, and when we shouted and applauded our approval, we realized that Ricky was actually embarrassed to talk. And so he didn't much.

The world opened up for Ricky through the use of sign language. And after his first year with us, his communication was a combination of simple signs and pantomime. We talked to him, and signed some. And when we really wanted to make an impression with him, we learned to SING, because Ricky loved music, and seemed to understand more easily the words we SANG.

I remember one special afternoon about six months after he came to us, listening to Bill Gaither's "Alleluia" on the living room stereo while I washed dishes in the kitchen. Suddenly I became aware of another voice accompanying the singers, and I peeked around the doorway. There stood Ricky in the middle of the room, hands reaching toward the ceiling, face tilted up, eyes closed, and he was SINGING "Ahh yae OOOO ya." I sat down on the carpet, leaned against the doorway, and wept my thanks for answers to prayer.

Progressively, Ricky became a wonderful communicator, using his own special mixture of pantomime, sign language and a few basic sounds. His silence was quite profound-- almost never totally silent, and always joyful – even musical, somehow. I still smile remembering the pantomimed stories he told me each day after school and his "comments" on the day. We worked hard to help him. He was "just one of the kids," and included in nearly every activity. He loved everyone who ever walked through the door, and ran a race to beat everyone else to the door when we heard the doorbell.

Every few months we returned to the medical specialists, wondering how he was doing with only one kidney, a "boot-shaped" heart, and limited hearing. We eventually got him a hearing aid, which helped with his receptive language. But before very long, for reasons we never completely understood, he got so frustrated with it that we were often fishing it out of trash cans, and when he eventually threw it under a lawn mower, we gave up on THAT idea!

One of my favorite Ricky stories was told me later by a friend, Glen. One day he saw Ricky riding his bicycle around our block. As Ricky pedaled toward the yard where he stood watering some flowers, Glenn noticed two older ladies sitting in a parked car along the side of the street facing Ricky's direction. Ricky saw them, too, pulled his bicycle alongside the front bumper of their car, and watched them watching him. After a few seconds, Ricky moved the bike closer to an open window, bent over, leaned inside and warmly hugged one of the startled women.

Then he straightened, waved goodbye, and rode off. Both women turned and watched him a few moments, then started their engine and drove slowly off in the opposite direction. Glen said Ricky waved at him as he peddled by, obviously satisfied with himself.

But as hard as we worked to help him become a more "appropriate" part of this world, he helped us be a part of another. For his was a world of such sweetness -- very unlike parts of this one.

I guess, looking back, I must believe that he was always just a visitor here. Doctors told us from the beginning that he was on "borrowed time," and that no one knew exactly how long he would be with us. But as he grew older and stronger, we began to make preparations for his future.

The summer he was almost 17, I began thinking about his future, and so decided to go confer with my parents and my father-in-law, about what they felt might be best. I rushed out the door of our house on the way to the airport one afternoon, heading to Nebraska for a week, and hurriedly hugged Ricky, along with my other kids, goodbye. He stood on the porch with the other kids, leaning against the white wooden porch support, waving goodbye as I drove off.

It was the last sight of him I would have. As I sat talking to my father-in-law the next day, Dad said, "Let's face it, Linda, Ricky's lived the best days of his life." And he assured me it had been a good one. A few hours later, my husband called me and said, "Ricky's gone. We've lost him." At first, I thought Ricky had wandered off on his bicycle again, and they couldn't find him. But through tears, Rod told me Ricky had drowned. And nothing in our family was quite the same again.

I remember Ricky running a race in the Special Olympics one sunny afternoon, years before. As he ran the short course with such joy, surrounded by some of his school friends, he kept his eyes not only on the course, but also searching the bleachers for me. When he spotted me, while trotting down the course, he gestured to me that he'd meet me "down there, okay?" and waved, "Hi, Mom!" It comforts my heart to know that wherever I go after the unique course set before me in this life, Ricky is already there waiting to give me the hug of "welcome home."

For the more than ten years he was ours, he taught us about love and forgiveness and joy. When he first came to us, the connection between action and language had not been bridged in his mind. It was if he had a short circuit or something. Language didn't mean much to him. We prayed for him all the time, that God would heal him, bring him language, and help us help him. One doctor told us that Ricky, it seemed to him, had been put together with spare parts because "nothing worked with anything else." Though they told us he would probably never reach adulthood, Ricky never gave up. He grew stronger and learned, and hugged nearly everyone he ever met.

I marveled at the size of his spirit. And as time went along, I realized that he was the one teaching us. He was the real giant among us —— the person who lived all the principles, or most of them, that theologians try to analyze and teach -- all of them. Ricky just WAS agape love, God's love, in our lives.

It was very difficult to let him go. As we said goodbye to him a few days later, Grandpa laid his palm on Ricky's chest and said, "You were a good boy, Ricky."

We buried him on John's birthday, and after the funeral, we all came home and spent time celebrating life with a small birthday party. We didn't really say it to each other, but I think that's what

Ricky was all about. He celebrated life, and the important things — especially love.

A few years later, after other great changes in our family, I dreamt one early morning that Ricky and I met together and talked in a beautiful light blue open space with no horizon. I remember telling him that I loved and missed him, and that I had wanted to be a good mother to him. He talked to me, telling me that he understood, and that he loved me, too. I don't know how long we spent together, or if it was a real meeting. It seemed so. All I know is that when I awoke, I could still feel the warmth of his arms around me, and a great calm comfort settled in my heart. It was more real then any dream I've ever had -- like a gift from God to help heal the hurting places still left in me.

By the way, I liked his voice!

How all of us loved being his family! How I loved being Ricky's mother, and how I thank God for the opportunity to "take a chance" with a "special child!"

CHAPTER 10

Surviving When You Don't Think You Can

Our family was forever changed by the life, and the death of a "special child."

You don't think as a parent, that your child could die. You try not to think of your kids becoming sick or hurt or dying. And then, if the very worst thing happens, you try to go on and make some sort of sense of it all, and sometimes that takes a long while.

Ricky died the end of June, and before the next September, I was once again, after a 17-year hiatus, teaching English, Drama and Speech in a nearby small high school as we continued on with the patterns of school and work for the family.

Ricky was rather like glue that held us together. His love and acceptance, and forever innocence infected us with acceptance and innocence and love we never knew we had.

Five years later, about two months after our divorce was finalized, very early one morning, I was awakened from a lovely dream by a ringing telephone. Is there anything more frightening than the telephone waking you in a dark room?

It was Melissa. She said, "Mom, I have to tell you something. John is dead. He was killed coming home from Sherman in his pickup late last night. He was driving. Randy was with him and is in the hospital. You'd better come."

John, at 25, separated from his one love, and the proud father of a tiny son. John had come to us at age 10, so frightened of being touched that he flinched whenever anyone reached to hug him. At first, he couldn't say how he really felt about much of anything. John trembled when he talked and people watched him, but he loved his big brother Randy, and his new younger brother, Kevin, and he had become instant buddies. And before long, he called us "Mom" and "Dad," asked to sit by me occasionally at meal times, just like the other kids, rested on my lap freely as we sat and talked around the table, and laughed and hugged. He had grown to play a guitar, write poetry, and live a sometimes lonely life. I had last seen him six months earlier when we just happened to cross paths in a movie parking lot in a town where neither of us lived. We had had a good visit that afternoon, parting with a hug and "I love you."

I had never felt free to invade his privacy. But now I wish that I had. There were so many things I should have said to him. So much I would have liked to help him understand, accept and overcome some of the obstacles in his life.

In between the deaths of my two sons, I had also buried a marriage. Actually, the divorce was formal recognition of an event that had occurred long before. The marriage hadn't exactly died – it just faded away, it seemed. It took several years after Ricky's death for the deep, though often unspoken division between my husband and me to completely unravel. I think it happened so slowly, neither of us knew what to do to fix anything. Knowing the risk of being rejected by well-intentioned people who didn't know anything about our struggles, I moved slowly and cautiously ahead. Eventually, we separated, and after more than 2 years in separate homes, we divorced. Someone once told me that there is really no such thing as an amicable divorce. I'm not sure about that, but I do believe that any divorce, however amicable, is sad and painful, especially for children.

I determined that we would do it with as much kindness and honor as possible, and I promised myself that whatever the future might bring, I would never do or say anything to intentionally undermine my children's love and respect for their dad. The family struggled for several years of hurt and loneliness, and I had moved about 7 hours away to get a "new start" with the twins, who were in Middle School. And now, several weeks after the divorce was finalized, John died.

The sense of loss was nearly overwhelming.

But we all came together and held each other, and cried together.

And we all survived.

We do that, you know. Somehow, we all survive.

I've been asked quite a number of times in the years since my sons died and my marriage ended for my "secrets" of surviving terrible hurts.

"You are such a strong person," people tell me. "How do you DO it?"

And so, I thought I'd best share with you some of the things I have learned through research, but mostly through experience. In many ways, once again, life itself is the very best teacher for those who want to "make sense of it all."

I remember telling my parents when I was young that I wanted to make my own mistakes and learn my own lessons. Since I was a particularly headstrong person, there wasn't much my parents could do to stop that sort of attitude after a certain age! I often learned lessons by paying the price for whatever choices I made, and my folks were great. They were loving, truthful, and supportive, but they usually let me suffer through the consequences of quite a number of REALLY DUMB choices!

And I did learn. Slowly, perhaps. But I did learn.

Do you not know trouble? It's a part of our world that we'd prefer getting rid of. When we're little, we dream of being grown up with our own home, family, car, great careers and absolutely no trouble! But life never really works that way, does it?

It isn't too far along in life, maybe by age six or seven, that we realize that sometimes people get sick, get poor, die, and sometimes people stop loving one another.

How does a person survive big, big hurts like that?

Where does one get the strength to go on when such pain is part of every moment??

Well, let me tell you a little about how it is for me.

To begin with, I think we survive and go on because we CHOOSE to.

Yes, that's right, we CHOOSE to go on.

I have told my friends and relatives this: "In life, you have two choices. Either you give up, or you grow." I've never been much of a person to quit in the middle of a tough situation. As long as there seems to be a slight chance of success, I usually try to hang in there. So, when I decide that I CAN survive the current emergency, I begin to believe and tell myself the GROWTH part.

When the burden of life's disappointments seem to be particularly heavy, I am reminded of the fact that in the physical world we increase our muscle strength by, on a regular basis, lifting increasingly heavier weights over a period of time. To increase our cardiovascular endurance, we walk and then jog on a regular basis, over increasingly longer paths.

With the passing of time, I realize that I am emotionally stronger today then I was a few years ago – not because I am older and people just naturally increase in emotional strength with time. Rather, my emotional and mental muscles have been stretched and strengthened by life. I'm stronger today because I've <u>had</u> to be in the past.

Actually, I'm not totally sure that the strength we're talking about comes ONLY as a result of practice. Experience certainly helps, but perhaps some of it comes in our genetic make up as well. And, of course, the patterns we see and hear about within our families.

I look at my biological daughters, particularly, and must note that the women in our family have, for several generations, modeled a certain resiliency, strength, and determination as noted in the patterns they have seen in the women that preceded them. My grandmother, in particular, was a tiny giant of a woman who accepted life, people, and her destiny with amazing strength and determination to continue meeting each day head-on. And she did for more than 104 years. I always pictured heel prints as the angels dragged her through the pearly gates! What grit!

Naturally, it does not surprise me to see similar characteristics growing in my daughters as well. In my family, we rather expect to live long and fully, and to survive storms, because that's what the women in our family DO! (And, as a sidelight, I believe the men in our family are often attracted to strong women, which is a positive for them, too!)

So, what if you might not have the sort of "survivor" background that is born in some people and developed in others? What would you do to develop a "survivor instinct?"

We could always go back to a scripture!

"… I have set before you life and death, the blessings and the curses; therefore choose life, that you and your descendants may live; and may love the Lord your God, obey His voice, and cling to Him. For He is your life and the length of your days, that you may dwell in the land which the Lord swore to give to your fathers, to Abraham,

Isaac and Jacob." (Deuteronomy 30:19-20 -- Amplified Version)

How about this one?

"Now set your mind and heart to seek (inquire of and require as your vital necessity) the Lord your God." (I Chronicles 22:19 -- Amplified Version)

Every day of our lives on this planet, you and I have the choice of the focus of our attention. We have the choice, Dear Ones, to believe in life and the good things of this world (as well as the next), or we may also choose to think badly of our own destiny and the destiny of the planet. Think about it.

Our world is filled with doomsday prophets who tell us how badly things are going, and who predict continued gloom ahead. You can listen to it and believe it if you choose. But I shall not.

I am determined to believe that there is as much beauty and goodness in the world as there ever was. I believe that mankind, and I, in particular, still have the ability to affect the world for good, and that all is not lost. Not yet! Not until the last moment of the last day should we give up!

Some people are like kids who stand, afraid, on the rail of a railroad train, hearing the whistle of the engine coming around a far turn. It doesn't take a BIG move to be safe. It just takes a step or two. But if they are waiting for someone else to do it for them, they will probably be surprised when rescue doesn't come to pull them off that track.

If I can see that I have an action in front of me that would help a situation, I act. I act with the confidence that if my intentions are pure, nothing will really destroy me. Of course, I can lose a battle. I can even lose my war, and my life. But even if that's the price tag, I WIN! Because dying is a gate we pass through to another life! And if I live through the battles ahead, I GROW and LEARN. If I don't live, I GO! And I KNOW that New Place

(Heaven) is going to be wonderful.

Perhaps you've seen t-shirts on some people that say proudly, "No Fear!" It's a good way to live if your heart and mind are unencumbered by fear and pain.

I know. Most of the time, that's how I live. Unafraid. Optimistic. Strong.

Not all the time. MOST of the time.

If life has dealt me a difficult hand, I continue to believe, somehow, the next hand will be better.

On the days when I am absolutely aching with grief or loneliness, I admit my pain to the Lord, and to myself. I shed my tears for a while, but not for long, and then I let my body and mind rest awhile.

Sometimes when I wrestle with unanswered questions, I choose to believe the answer will eventually come. And, again, I rest. If the problem or pain on my mind is something for which I <u>know</u> I cannot find a quick answer, then I generally allow myself only a limited time to dwell on it. I consciously set aside the "issues" I cannot solve. I lay down, focus my mind on some unimportant thing, like a magazine article, or a television program, and when my mind is quiet, I go to sleep, trusting the Lord to bring peace to my mind while my body rests for a little while.

It has become increasingly amazing to me that when I rest with confidence, the answers I have sought often come to me in the quiet sleep or near sleep. Often, the answers have a clarity and rightness that I could never have found under my own steam. God works with me during those quiet times when I've "done all" and stand (or rest!).

Over the years, I have also developed the ability to "wait," and anyone who knows me for any length of time will tell you that I am not a natural waiter! This one, or as much of the gift as I have so far developed, has come through difficult trial and error. When there is nothing you can do to feel stronger or better or smarter or happier, WAIT. As patiently as possible. As confidently as possible. Remember that things change, and if I don't have the strength to deal with this situation today, or the wisdom to find the answers I need, the day will come when I will.

I have also learned to wait for grief to lift. Once I allow myself to actually experience and admit my loss, there is a time of healing. I do not hang on to the pain like an old companion. I do not enjoy its company, and I do not intentionally feed it well, with anger and bitterness and despair. I do allow it to leave. But the going is sometimes a slow, quiet process.

Along the way, each day, I try to keep my heart honest and clean of any leftover anger, unforgiveness or bitterness. About much of anything. Anger, unforgiveness, or bitterness are like cobwebs in the corners of our mind that reach out and trap grief and sickness. Cleaning those feelings out of our conscious mind on a regular basis can do much to speed healing, bring hope and encourage peace of mind.

I believe that I have the God-given destiny to live in all the abundance promised to the children of God in Scripture – not because I deserve a good life any more than anyone else, but because God promised it to His kids. That includes ME! And, God doesn't lie.

When I die, I will leave my few earthly possessions to my children, hopefully to be shared equally, or as nearly as possible, by each of them, all the things that I have worked to acquire. Not because my kids are equally loving or responsive to me, or that they actually have accomplished any particular thing to deserve the inheritance. I give to them because I love them, and because all I am or have belongs to them. It's part of their heritage.

If I, as selfish and shortsighted as I might be, want to share with the children I have loved, how more certain am I that my heavenly Father has good things for me in His treasure chest!

And so I shall believe in the goodness promised me, in an abundant life, in the strength to meet the challenges of each day, and the ability to survive.

When difficult times hit us, the first question that seems to come up is, "Why me? What have I done to deserve this?"

I have come to believe that God is perfectly wise and wonderful, and He knows that sometimes it is better for me to be challenged, for me to face difficult times. I don't always immediately (or ever!) understand the whys of this. Probably never will. But I trust that my Father isn't mad at me, and that He still loves me, and that I will grow as a result of the problems of my life. I didn't necessarily consciously choose today's problem. But I have planted a few really dumb seeds by my thoughts, fears and actions, so may have begun the operation that produced today's junk.

With every challenge, I have the choice to give up or grow. Occasionally, when I feel that determination to grow beginning to weaken and waver, I go to a quiet place and spend some time alone with my Father, asking Him for a bigger portion of whatever he thinks I need — wisdom, courage, strength, forgiveness, understanding. Some people call this time prayer. Others use the term meditation. Whatever you call it, it's a private time, and very, very honest.

When I ask Him for help, I expect that peace and hope will return to me once again. Maybe not in a quick moment, but certainly, quietly, before very long, I find myself able to continue on.

Growing.

Learning.

Being.

CHAPTER 11

Wrapping It All Up with Love

For more than the last 40 years of my life, I chose to center much of my thoughts, prayers and activities on the extended family given to me by marriage, birth, adoptions, foster care, church, prayer, teaching, friendship, counseling, and assorted miracles of "divine connection." For the most part, it has been the most joyful of experiences.

Along the way, my children gave me the freedom and encouragement to go to school, return to full-time teaching, part-time writing, and to find my own path to individual fulfillment. And they have shared their lives with part-time writer/philosopher, counselor, dreamer, artist, and full-time Mom, with great kindness and consideration.

I believe I have been a good mom. Not perfect. But good. I believe I have often put their needs first in my life. And as I look back, I can honestly say that I regret only a few of my decisions.

Certainly, to date, the greatest joy of my life has been being "Mom," and now "Nana" to so many neat kids. Each child and each memory of that child that still lives in me is a source of great pride and satisfaction.

All of these individuals today are people I'd be proud to have you meet. Each of them is a unique, interesting, marvelous adult.

I know that I have not told them often enough that I am proud of them. I know that I have not told them often enough that I love them more than peanut butter and chocolate.

It is a freeing thing to do that now.

Melissa, you have such wonderful strength, such a determination, joy and beauty. I'm proud of your ambitions. And such tenacity! I should have named you "honesty" because you nearly always speak the truth, and mostly with love. No wonder you help people get well so easily. You've been helping me be well all your life. I absolutely adore you. When I hear your voice, see your smile, or feel your heartfelt hugs, I feel pretty doggoned proud of myself for being your mom.

Kevin, I hug a big man in my arms, and remember the darling boy who lives inside, the one with a giant heart to match his great big smile. I still hear that freckle-faced little boy running through the front door after school, yelling, "Hey, Mom! What's to eat!?" I marvel at your creative talents. When you hurt, you big man, I hurt, too. Always have. Always will. When you grin, the sun shines and my world is brighter.

Katie, my own precious Kathryn, who is also so much me, I remember your patience and kindness with your little brothers as you "taught" them. What a passionate soul! Strong, beautiful, stubborn, creative, determined, and smart in so many ways. But more. Even when the path you've chosen becomes steeper or rougher, like your Mom, you keep going. So keep on growing and learning, Darling. Oh, I'm also proud that you're a great mother!

Randy, who came to me almost grown. Then you were a man in a boy's body in many ways. Later, for awhile, you became a boy again. Now, dear son, you've grown into a lovely man and a wonderful father for your daughters, often through trying times and great distance. You've been wonderfully loyal to all your family, and I've enjoyed seeing your pride in becoming a grandfather. You often think with your heart, and when you told me a few years ago, "I choose YOU," I was thrilled, because I choose YOU, too.

Kathy, you've a heart that is absolutely pure in so many wonderful ways. No matter where you are, or what has happened to you, you seem to forgive and go on. I wish each day that I could make your life all you would like it to be, because you deserve good things, my dear girl. I love you, always.

Andrew, I believe you have the kindest heart of us all, though you work so hard to not let anyone know it. I want the best for you, my darling boy, and miss you when I don't hear from you. I look forward to the day you bring home that special someone who will love you completely, who will see the goodness in you that I see, and will help you be all you want to be in life.

David, so private with your feelings, so strong, so determined and focused, and yet so gentle with your daughter, and so good to the rest of your family. I believe you can be anything you set your mind to become. The last few years of your adolescence, you were the center of much of my life, and I loved it. Now you are grown, and I like it that we are friends. I'm proud of your life choices and the way you take care of others. Wherever I go, whatever happens, know there will always be room for you in my heart, and at my table!

John, gone now. I still can't believe it. Loving you was very easy, John. So quiet and hiding inside that beautiful shell was such a good person. I wish I'd have understood more about helping you talk about feelings when you were younger. I'm glad the last things we said to each other were words of love. Your son Jeremy is beautiful. Grown now, he still has your eyes. You'd be so proud of him with his baby boy. Because Jeremy is here, we still feel we have you, too.

Ricky, you taught me how to love. I think I may miss you most of all. I never really understood religious principles until I knew you. Things like Agape love, forgiveness, joy and friendship were just words until you became my son. I believe that you must be tending the gates of heaven, welcoming newcomers just as you welcomed everyone to our house here on earth. And you were there to hug John and Grandpa, who followed you to heaven. I'll love you for all eternity for teaching me, even without words, great truths, and fabulous love.

The greatest thing I ever did in my life was being a Mom.

CHAPTER 12

"Miracles in the Making"

Time in the shape of moments, months and even years have passed since I first began writing about our family. We've seen graduations, weddings, births, deaths, divorces, and all the variety of life experiences common to man. There are new members of our immediate family, and we've lost several very precious people. A second wave of grandchildren, have been arriving the last few years, and I'm even a great-grandmother. This past year, we lost baby granddaughter, Sophia, as well as my dear Tammy, who wanted to model her mom years after me.

Our family continues to evolve, grow, and rearrange itself. And I continue to grow and to learn, many times in the middle of the great, wonderful chaos of our coming together.

I originally thought this work was meant to be read by my own children, grandchildren, and perhaps a few others. However, after so many years of teaching, and of loving other people's kids, too, I realize that there are many things I cannot express in a classroom to the young people who are rushing, often without a thought, into relationships, marriage and parenting. And some of these ideas need to be taught, somehow. At the very least, they need to be made available.

Our society has changed in many ways since I first began teaching high school classes in the fall of 1966. We have moved into a progressively technological world, trusting science and computers, cell phones, and electronic security systems, to watch over and teach our children. Parenting seems to have moved from "hands on" to "hands off." Sadly, public education attempts to fill in the missing components, and with each year, it becomes more obvious that we are missing some important principles about "training up a child." Today, the need to protect, encourage and teach some basic truths to young American families is probably as important, or perhaps MORE important than ever.

As this manuscript comes to a close, I realize that some of my ideas are far from "politically correct" in this time of fearful name calling and blind, self-centered empowerment. However, that does not keep the ideas I carry to this table from being true. And though our culture seems to be heading down some mighty slippery slopes, I still believe that hope is not lost and miracles can happen. God is still watching us with love, and He waits for us to ask for His help, His order for the family.

Over these many years, I have seen some wonderful and unexplainable things happen. And because of this, my faith has grown stronger in a God Who not only cares about us, but sometimes miraculously intervenes in our lives. So, when you need the help, ask. He's waiting with your miracle. I believe it. I've lived it.

I am privileged to have known and loved "official" children who called me "Mom." They grew into interesting and strong adults, and most of them still like to hug and talk with me from time to time. There have been numerous moments through the years when I KNOW God was watching over us, caring for each of us. And one of these days, I'll begin telling those stories. But for now, the miracle that fills my heart is remembering all that love, all that laughter, all that laundry (!) and all the joy of having been there, having done that!

God Bless.

LaVergne, TN USA
26 October 2009
161988LV00001B/2/P